Voices from the Valley

FSG Originals × *Logic*

FARRAR, STRAUS AND GIROUX

New York

Voices
from the
Valley

Tech Workers Talk About
What They Do—and How They Do It

*Edited by Ben Tarnoff
and Moira Weigel*

FSG Originals × *Logic*
Farrar, Straus and Giroux
120 Broadway, New York 10271

Library of Congress Cataloging-in-Publication Data
Names: Tarnoff, Ben, editor. | Weigel, Moira, 1984– editor.
Title: Voices from the Valley : tech workers talk about what they
     do—and how they do it / edited by Ben Tarnoff and Moira
     Weigel.
Description: First edition. | New York : FSG Originals × *Logic* ;
     Farrar, Straus and Giroux, 2020.
Identifiers: LCCN 2020018717 | ISBN 9780374538675
     (paperback)
Subjects: LCSH: High technology industries—California—Santa
     Clara Valley (Santa Clara County)—Employees—Interviews. |
     Service industries workers—California—Santa Clara Valley
     (Santa Clara County)—Interviews.
Classification: LCC HD8039.H542 C222 2020 | DDC
     331.7/660979473—dc23
LC record available at https://lccn.loc.gov/2020018717

Our books may be purchased in bulk for promotional,
educational, or business use. Please contact your local bookseller
or the Macmillan Corporate and Premium Sales Department at
1-800-221-7945, extension 5442, or by e-mail at
MacmillanSpecialMarkets@macmillan.com.

www.fsgoriginals.com • www.fsgbooks.com • www.logicmag.io
Follow us on Twitter, Facebook, and Instagram at @fsgoriginals
and @logic_magazine

10 9 8 7 6 5 4 3 2 1

Francesca Leonardi

Edited by Ben Tarnoff and Moira Weigel
Voices from the Valley

Ben Tarnoff is the author of the books *The Bohemians: Mark Twain and the San Francisco Writers Who Reinvented American Literature* and *A Counterfeiter's Paradise: The Wicked Lives and Surprising Adventures of Three Early American Moneymakers* and is a cofounder of *Logic* magazine. His writing has appeared in *The Guardian*, *The New Republic*, *Jacobin*, and *Lapham's Quarterly*, among other publications. He lives in Cambridge, Massachusetts.

Moira Weigel is the author of the book *Labor of Love: The Invention of Dating*. Her writing has appeared in *The New York Times*, *The Atlantic*, *The New Yorker*, *The Guardian*, *The Nation*, *The New Republic*, and *n+1*, among other publications, and she is a cofounder of *Logic* magazine. She is a Junior Fellow at Harvard University and lives in Cambridge, Massachusetts.

Also by Ben Tarnoff

The Bohemians: Mark Twain and the San Francisco Writers
Who Reinvented American Literature

A Counterfeiter's Paradise: The Wicked Lives and Surprising
Adventures of Three Early American Moneymakers

Also by Moira Weigel

Labor of Love: The Invention of Dating

Contents

■ ■ ■

Voices from the Valley

Introduction: The Everyone Machine

This book is a tell-all about an open secret: platforms are made by people. For many people, it can be easy to miss.

There is the matter of word choice. "Platform" instead of "publisher." "AI" instead of "statistics." Tech companies have many reasons to speak as if their products run themselves.

To obscure the human work involved in training an algorithm or moderating a social media feed is both a sales pitch and an evasion. The pitch, for investors, is scale: a tech company will grow at superhuman speed. The evasion is of liability: a tech company will not be held responsible for what it breaks by moving this fast. For users, this is part of the promise, too: no gatekeepers, just a frictionless exchange of ideas, goods, and services. May the best meme win. *Pay no attention to that man inside the black box!*

This book will introduce you to the people behind the platforms. These are people whose work, in one way or another, shapes almost everything you do—how you find a job or a lover, get approved for a loan or flagged for a police stop, rave about a movie or fight about a president. In recent years, the power of the major tech companies has become impossible to ignore. For the first time, many politicians and pundits are attacking them as monopolies that inflict a wide range of harms on society, from promoting fake news and hate speech to eroding our privacy and attention spans. And as moments of conflict or crisis arise in some companies, dissidents and other malcontents have spoken up: leaking audio and screenshots, talking to reporters, walking out on the job. But it remains relatively rare to hear the ordinary people at those companies talk in ordinary ways about what they do. In this book they'll speak to you in their own words.

One set of voices you will hear belongs to tech's most privileged caste: the full-time employees (FTEs). These are the people whom bestsellers mean when they ask, *Are you smart enough to work at Google?* They traverse the San Francisco Peninsula in company buses with tinted windows.

Their employers are notoriously secretive. Their offices sit behind many layers of security. A host of services—cafeterias, laundries, fitness studios—keep them on campus. Many of them went to school together; many of them date one another. Some of them get married.

The tightness of the social networks they inhabit imposes high costs on sharing anything with outsiders. In case these costs are not enough of a deterrent, the FTEs have also signed a nondisclosure agreement. *For the purposes of this Agreement, confidential information includes all information that your employer treats with confidentiality.* You can't enter an office of a major tech company without signing a promise to take any code you might see on a screen, diagram on a whiteboard, or slogan on a wall with you to the grave. BE OPEN, the walls of Facebook read.

Most tech companies pride themselves on the free flow of information among their employees. But they insist that it stay there. As a result, media coverage of tech has historically followed a few scripts. It was never hard to find gadget reviews or business reporting—to figure out what to buy your stepdad for Christmas or how much a startup raised in its Series B. But journalists trying to tell a deeper story quickly ran into the wall of the NDA. There, they often found they had to make do with what industry PR gave them.

When it came to executives, founders, people at the top, what PR encouraged was hagiography. Many reporters took the bait: the paeans to Steve Jobs, who was pictured presenting the first iPhone in the posture of Leonardo da Vinci's *Salvator Mundi*, were only the most on the nose. The fact that the people at the top were the only ones allowed to talk to the media reinforced the idea that they spoke for everyone.

When it came to the rank and file, it was hard to get anyone on record. Mostly, you heard whispers of extravagant and eccentric lifestyles: kombucha on tap at the campus cafeteria and kale at the poké bar, weekends spent microdosing before participating in meticulously planned orgies and other forms of rationalized libertinism—tales from a smartwatch world in which the only taboo left was wasting time.

I want you to make our readers hate themselves, one magazine editor told a friend he had commissioned to write a story about the perks that tech companies were using to lure recruits.

Not long after, he left the magazine to go write copy for a tech company.

⁘

Not everyone in tech gets the perks, of course. In this book, in addition to FTEs, you will hear from another group of people: contractors. Historically, the media has ignored them. But the industry needs them to function.

This large and ever-shifting category includes people whose jobs have always been outsourced. They drive the shuttles with the tinted windows; they guard the entrance to HQ and cook the food and serve the coffee to keep the engineers working late. But increasingly, tech companies are also outsourcing what used to be full-time roles.

Many white-collar workers like recruiters and designers are now contractors, too. Elsewhere, invisible masses perform new kinds of digital piecework, like labeling data to train machine-learning algorithms or taking down videos that violate a platform's terms of service.

Contractors are a fast-growing percentage of the overall tech workforce: at Google, for instance, they constitute the majority. They often endure low wages and difficult working conditions. Nonetheless, many of them also take pride in their craft.

The tech industry places a premium on "technical" skills. But one recurring theme of our conversations is that *all* work involves technique, whether it is preparing steak for several hundred people or massaging bodies that hours of coding have turned into slabs of concrete.

The contractors in this book have some of the deepest insights into the tech industry and the deepest roots in the Bay Area. They remember the last bubble—the way it changed the landscape and their neighborhoods, the lavish lawns that newly minted millionaires planted and the friends who had to move away so that their homes could be demolished to make space for conference hotels.

Journalists and scholars are starting to pay more attention to more of the people who make up the tech industry. This book aims to give you a fuller picture of their lives, by letting them explain where they came from and why, what they do and what they still hope to do. It also shows how their lives intersect. This book aspires to be representative. It is not exhaustive. It could not be, because Silicon Valley is now everywhere.

Every city wants to have a tech hub. Silicon Beach,

Silicon Alley, Silicon Hills, and Silicon Desert—these are ones you may have heard of. Countless other aspirants have not made it as far. But all over the world, politicians and businesspeople are trying to replicate the legendary ecosystem of Northern California. Silicon Valley has long seemed like the last refuge of the American dream.

By the same token, every company wants to be a tech company. JPMorgan Chase employs fifty thousand technologists, two-thirds of whom are software engineers. That's more engineers than are employed by many big tech firms. Does that make JPMorgan Chase a tech company? The boundaries are becoming difficult to draw.

We still talk about "the" tech industry. But increasingly, tech is a layer of every industry. One by one, farms and factories and oil fields are becoming "smart." As we reap what we sow, sensors feed data about the seasons into the cloud.

You, too, are being fed to the cloud. As tech enters every industry, it is also entering every aspect of life. Platforms are not only made *by* people. They are made *of* people—including you.

It has become almost impossible to avoid being a source of data. You can stay off social media and shop local, and maybe you should. But, as you make your way to the café to meet your old friend, your phone will ping the nearest cell towers. Leave your phone at home, and the security camera on your neighbor's house will capture your face and relay it to Amazon.

Speak, whoever you are. Your voice is in the Valley, too.

1

The Founder

In Silicon Valley, the founder is a sacred figure. Starting a business is seen as the highest form of human achievement. Most startups fail, of course. For the founder, however, failure is never a source of shame. Rather, there is something ennobling about it.

Yet this reverence for the founder feels increasingly untethered from the realities of the industry. Silicon Valley is no longer a scrappy place, if it ever was. It is a land of giants, and their appetite for startups is immense. Huge corporations are constantly acquiring their smaller competitors, or companies that might someday grow into their competitors. This is not only to protect their position, but to nab some of those revered founders themselves, in the hopes that regular infusions of entrepreneurial blood will keep them young and nimble. They, too, were startups once.

We spoke to a founder who cut a successful path through the ecosystem. This person learned to code, landed at an elite university with deep links to tech, became a founder, and failed upward into a company that was too big to fail. Yet along the way, the founder grew disillusioned. Successes started to feel more like failures. Silicon Valley started to feel strange.

✻

How did you start writing code?

I went to a perfectly fine public school in Texas. We had a computer science course, but the teacher didn't know anything about programming. We had a textbook, though, and if you were sufficiently self-motivated, you could work through the exercises and then take the AP exam. Fortunately, there were a few of us who really liked to code. So we got together and taught the course ourselves. We all passed the exam, and it helped me get into an elite institution for college.

What did arriving at that elite institution look like?

It was weird. There was a big cultural gap.

I resented my family for not having prepared me for the experience. There were all these kids who went to private schools who were years ahead of me in math. I was angry that I didn't get those opportunities, and that came out as resentment toward my parents for a while.

I remember going to my college girlfriend's parents' house and feeling intimidated by the food they ate and the way they talked. But I also knew I wanted to emulate it. Throughout college, I put a lot of pressure on myself to make sure that nobody could say I wasn't supposed to be there. That was the particular form that impostor syndrome took for me: it wasn't about the fear of not being a good programmer, but the fear of not belonging.

The path that college put me on created some distance between me and my parents, though. They have never been anything but proud of me, but they stopped understanding me sometime in college. And in the years since, the gaps between our worlds continue to grow wider.

To this day, when I call my mom on the weekend, she still asks me if I'm off that day, because she doesn't know that people only work Monday through Friday in offices. That's just not context that she has—and I didn't have it, either, before I left for college. My stepdad says if I ever wanted to move back home I could find work because there's a local guy who fixes computers.

Apart from the culture shock, what was college like?
The school where I went wasn't friendly to failure. It was a meat grinder. When you walked through campus around finals week you saw kids sitting on the ground crying.

Still, it's the kind of place where you make connections that end up mattering a lot later. You meet people who will go on to start companies in Silicon Valley, or who will become higher-ups at bigger firms. It's also the kind of place where recruiters track you from freshman year, have dinner with you at department-sponsored events—that sort of thing.

That industry interest made me feel special. And when I became a teaching assistant for a computer science course, that interest intensified. I had to do a work-study as part of my financial aid, and it was either serving food in the cafeteria or teaching computer science. But teaching paid well—fifteen dollars an hour, which blew my mind, since my high school job had paid four dollars an hour plus tips.

Plus the job was super fun, and the industry attention felt great. Big firms would come in and lavish the teaching assistants with gifts—embarrassing gifts. Sometimes we would go buy cheap tricycles and ride them down a steep hill and play a sort of human *Mario Kart*. Microsoft found out about it and bought us the highest-quality tricycles available. I think it's actually gotten worse since I've left. These days companies send stretch Hummer limos to pick kids up for fancy dinners.

So you must've been pretty well set up for a job in tech by the time you graduated.
After I graduated I had a few options of places to work. I chose an older, more established company. That ended up being one of the worst decisions I've ever made in my life. I spent two years there while my friends were jumping on rocket ships. Then I decided to start a startup with somebody I knew from school.

My cofounder and I had been talking for several months about doing our own thing. In college, everybody was expected to go start a startup—that expectation had been drilled pretty deep into us. We lived in a big house with a bunch of friends, and we turned an extra room into an office. We had a really nice routine. We worked there every day, and tried to prototype things very quickly.

This was around 2009, when mobile apps were taking off. It was the era of "SoLoMo"—"social local mobile." The iPhone had changed everything: there had been programming platforms for phones before, but they were garbage. Everyone wanted to build something for the App Store. The tech giants were way behind the curve, however— the Facebook mobile app was horrible, for example. It seemed possible that the bigger players just weren't going to make it on mobile, and that created opportunities for startups like us.

So we tried to build a bunch of different apps. None of them found a huge amount of success. But the last one we tried, a social app for making plans with friends, did well enough to get some attention from *TechCrunch* and other places in the tech press.

It was fun, but scary. Because we always knew that if one of the tech giants got their shit together, they could eat our lunch if they wanted to. I remember waking up one day and seeing a new product announcement from Facebook that I was convinced would put us out of business. I ran to my cofounder's room, freaking out. It turned out we were fine. Still, I had that feeling of "Holy shit, we're fucked" a lot. We lived in constant fear of getting scooped.

But you didn't.
Not exactly. But after a year, we were still living off our savings. It was clear that we either needed to get funding, get a job, or get acquired.

Around this time, we went to an up-and-coming company to ask them whether they would give us access to their private API.* They said, essentially, "No way. You're a tiny company that doesn't matter." But they also said they'd be interested in acquiring us. We were very surprised to hear that. We didn't even really know what it meant. But we decided to pursue it.

What they were offering is what Silicon Valley calls a "talent acquisition." They wanted to buy the company, but they weren't going to take our technology. They weren't going to take our code. They just wanted to get the two of us working for them. They put me and my cofounder through an interview process, and it was the same standard interview process I'd already been through before. But at the end of it, they made an offer with a slightly different format. It was clear that we were talking to people who worked in their M&A [mergers and acquisitions] department rather than in recruiting. Those people have the authority to write bigger checks, and they're supposed to be thinking about what the company is going to need a little further down the line.

We were very green, so we didn't know what a good offer looked like. But we did know that we should go get at least one competing offer, to see what our options were. So, using our network of contacts from college, we reached out to somebody who had the ear of a few VPs at a bigger company that made similar acquisition

---

* API stands for "application programming interface." It is an agreement that governs how programs talk to one another over the internet. In this case, access to the company's private API would mean the ability to obtain and use some of its data.

offers. We said, "Hey, we have this offer from one of your competitors. They're moving fast. Can we start a conversation with you?"

Recruiters famously don't make the process very fast for people. You can do an interview and not hear back for a month, for instance. It's frustrating for most people coming in the front door. But it's very different if you have an offer from a competitor. An offer from a competitor is always the best way to get their attention, even if they have ignored you in the past. And doubly so through the M&A route.

How old were you at the time?
Twenty-three. This was all very new to me. Even with some experience in the industry, I had no idea how corporations worked. No one in my family worked for a corporation.

So we went into the bigger company and did a presentation for several directors. They found it interesting, because we were thinking about the same problems that they needed to be thinking about. Because the big companies missed the boat on mobile, they were willing to write checks to make up for that gap. That's probably the biggest phase of talent acquisition that I've seen in my career. Although maybe today acquisitions around AI could rival it.

They liked our product enough to make an offer. Their offer was many multiples larger than the first one we'd received. They were a larger company, with more money to spend. They were also more frightened of smaller competitors outmaneuvering them, so they were willing to spend more.

They wanted to acquire all of the assets of our company for a particular price and then wind the company down. The price they proposed was pretty high. And being a young kid with lots of student loan debt, I was blown away by the seriousness of that number. That's the main thing I remember.

How did they decide how much the assets were worth?
It was a charade. Our assets weren't actually worth anything. We had a negligible number of users. Our service was not wildly popular by any means. So they valued the assets pretty arbitrarily—this chunk of code is worth this many millions of dollars.

You said the smaller company wanted to acquire you as a way to hire you and your cofounder, but wasn't interested in your technology or your code. What about the bigger company?
They were planning to throw away every line of code. There was nothing that they were actually acquiring besides us.

Then why buy your code if they're just going to throw it away? Wouldn't it have been easier to just hire you, instead of hiring you *and* buying your code?
Sometimes the big tech companies acquire startups to acquire their technology, and sometimes they do it just to

prevent those startups from becoming competitors. In our case, it was the latter.

Even if a big company is not directly threatened by a startup as a competitor currently, the thinking is that if they need to buy them later, they're going to pay a lot more for it. So they might as well buy the startup as early as possible to nip it in the bud. Our startup was pre-funding, so they could get away with paying us much less. We didn't have any investors they had to satisfy.

But acquiring our assets was also a way to justify paying us a lot. If they're only going to pay you two times the normal salary, then that can take the form of a very nice job offer. But if they're going to pay you more like eight or ten times, it breaks the whole idea of salary bands, which is how big companies organize compensation by experience level. So buying your assets is the back door—it's a way to get away with paying certain people much more.

As far as what they're buying—yes, they're avoiding paying more for a potential competitor later. But the inherent value in a talent acquisition comes from acknowledging that most projects in software fail. Finding a team that can actually ship something that gets out the door is rare. Even at big companies, most projects will not see the light of day. So to find a group of people that have managed to build something—even if it's small, even if it's humble—means they're probably a team that works well together. So they're worth a premium. That's the theory behind it, at least.

Also, they could make us sign a contract that locked us in for a long time. The deal to acquire our startup was a lump of cash and a job offer. We had to take both to-gether. About half of the payment came up front, in the form of the cash. And the rest would come to us through salary and stock-based compensation on a vesting sched-ule over the course of four years.

Sure, I could've showed up on day one and quit. And they would've been angry at me, but I still would've been able to pay off my student loans. However, I would've been leaving a lot of money on the table.

Were you excited? Paying off your student loans must've felt pretty good.

I was very excited and very terrified. I didn't want to screw it up. The deal was complicated. There were hundreds of pages of legal documents that I felt very overwhelmed by. We had to pay a lawyer fifty thousand dollars to make sure everything was airtight. My parents didn't under-stand it, and to this day don't understand it. My friends in tech were happy—some of them had been through this experience before.

But it changed my life. I went from being basically broke—my next rent payment would have emptied out my savings account, not to mention my student loans—to not having to worry about money anymore. So that was great.

How did it feel to go from running a startup to working for a big company?

It was intimidating, but there were some really positive aspects. As an engineer, I learned a lot. I felt like I was finally learning how to actually write software. I would go home and read the company's internal wikis for hours. I was so excited about working there that I read documentation every weekend for a year, actually.

But coming in as a talent acquisition, you're also expected to be a thought leader. You're expected to inject the company with new ideas. It's an informal role—it's not reflected in your title. But that's why management has paid a premium for you.

So my cofounder and I started to materialize what we thought this company needed, and assembled a team of people to work on it. The fact that we could come in and substantially change product direction—that we could create and staff and launch a project—was due to the fact that the company had paid extra for us. Leadership assumed we knew something.

Failing Up, Down, and Sideways

**You said that most projects in software fail.
Why is that?**
Because you never know what's going to work. Market timing is everything: something that makes perfect sense two years from now, or made sense two years *ago*, might fail today for no good reason. Everything changes so fast: the technology stack, consumer demand, even the fundamental capabilities of these devices.

I mean, everything I've ever worked on has failed.

I've worked on some ambitious projects at several of these big companies, and none of them have succeeded. But I've still been rewarded and promoted. And I think that's a good thing about Silicon Valley. Failure isn't looked down upon, which is a positive aspect of tech culture.

When you fail inside a big company, does it still *feel* like failure?

The average time spent on a team is well under two years at most of these big companies. So when a company wants to change direction and abandon a product, people usually don't take it that hard because they weren't planning on being there for very long anyway.

On some teams, however, that's not the case. I'm currently on a team that has been working on something for several years. And it's failing. We have been launching small representative parts of our product, but users aren't using them.

This is partly a problem with what constitutes success within a big company: if you launch a product with a million users, it'll get killed because a million users is nothing. That's one of the reasons that big companies have trouble innovating, because achieving a 1 percent gain in users of your main product will win every time over launching a new product with a much smaller user base. I mean, a million users would be a rocket ship success for an early startup. For a big company, it's a drop in the bucket. That's why big companies tend to get stagnant, because they'll always prioritize growing the main product over funding experimental ventures.

Anyway, on my team, failure has really depleted our energy. We're demoralized because we've been grinding for a long time on something that just isn't taking off. It used to be one of the best teams I've ever been on—but within a period of six months, we've become very unproductive. We have no direction.

That sounds like burnout.
People get burned-out not because they're working too hard but because they're not feeling rewarded by the work they're doing. They get burned-out because they believe their work has no impact. On my team, since we know it's only a matter of time before leadership kills our product, people are burning out left and right.

At work, there are certain things you have to do. But what the company is really paying you for is to come up with new things to do. They're paying for your creativity. When I'm burned-out, I'm still doing the things I have to do—I'm filing the TPS reports—but I'm not coming up with new things to do.* Burnout is when the creative part of your work is dead. There's a muscle I go to flex and it's just not there.

---

* The mention of TPS reports is a reference to the movie *Office Space* (1999), where they represent pointless, and mandatory, paperwork.

What about in the startup world? Failure must look different inside a startup.

If you launch a startup that goes out of business, no one thinks you wasted your time. People still revere a founder whose company has failed, even to a fault. Plus, because there's always more money being pumped into tech, it's a soft landing for almost anyone whose startup fails.

That changes depending on what you're working on and the time period, of course. For instance, I don't think if your social app failed today you would have a nice acquisition offer waiting for you, unless you knew the potential acquirers on a personal level. And that ends up being the major way that the opportunities for "failing upward" are not distributed equally.

Who is allowed to fail, and who gets to fail upward? Your startup wasn't failing, exactly, but it sounds like the people you met in college were the determining factor in your ability to land acquisition offers.

Definitely. In our case, that was the main thing. We didn't have an impressive piece of technology or an impressive user base. But we did have social capital.

There are other ways to accrue social capital. If your startup gets press attention, that raises its acquisition price. If you have a really stellar team, that's another way to fail upward. You could assemble a dozen excellent engineers to work on a very hard problem and then fail at that problem. But you found a dozen engineers that can work together without killing each other and maybe even manage to ship something. That's worth a lot.

On the one hand, Silicon Valley seems to revere entrepreneurialism. On the other hand, the industry is increasingly dominated by a handful of big companies—companies that, as you've explained, frequently acquire startups and burn down all their assets to ensure they don't become competitors. How do you make sense of that contradiction between the cult of the founder and the increasingly monopolistic structure of tech?

The funding model for startups is venture capital. And venture capital is a hits-driven business: you expect the vast majority of your investments to fail, so the ones that succeed have to succeed on a massive scale. Venture capital is risky, and it requires a lot of money.

Until relatively recently, tech companies didn't have enough money to compete with venture capitalists. But now they do. Today, you have four or five tech giants with cash piles big enough to really push people around. And this has only happened in the last decade or so—it wasn't like that in the early 2000s after the first dot-com crash.

But the incentives of a VC firm are different from those of a tech giant, right? The former is giving you capital to help you grow into a bigger company, whereas the latter is buying you to make sure you *don't* grow into a bigger company.

Right. But again, the tech giant is also buying you because you're a founder who has had some amount of success. The reverence for the founder might sound silly, but it's based on something real, which is that it's really hard to measure *why* a company is successful.

There are too many factors at play: market timing, staffing decisions, choices about the technology stack. It's impossible to know why a particular startup succeeds. So you find something to control for, and that's the people. That's why big tech companies like to bet on founders. This is something I've noticed in my career: there are people who are just very effective, and the things they touch seem to work. And most people aren't like that.

How have your views of the acquisition experience, and of the tech industry more broadly, changed over time?
I felt I was succeeding while the acquisition was happening. I had worked hard and I was being rewarded for it. The system was working.

But today I look back and think of it as a failure. Why didn't I work on something more challenging? Why didn't I take a bigger swing? At the time, I thought I was working on something groundbreaking. Now, with some hindsight and maturity, I think I just got lucky doing something small.

I definitely feel like this was a silly chapter in my life. I'm very glad I got to pay off my student loans. But I don't feel good about the work. In fact, I feel pretty embarrassed about it.

It's not that I consider myself a failure for not having built a successful business. The failure I feel is more personal: it's that I spent my time on building a small social app instead of something that would have been more meaningful.

What would've been more meaningful?
I could have worked on something that actually had a positive impact on society. Or I could've set out to solve a problem that had more interesting technology behind it.

Making the World a Better Place

What do you think changed your mind? Because you didn't feel that way at first.
I think it was seeing more of the industry, spending time at these big companies, and observing certain things.

One of those had to do with bias. Silicon Valley has been under attack for the past several years for having a lot of bias in its compensation practices around gender and race. As a result, the big companies have tried to standardize the way they pay people. They'll break compensation into salary bands that are supposed to match an employee's level. So if you're at a certain level, your pay falls somewhere within the corresponding salary band. Which means that if a man and a woman are in the same band, they're going to be paid roughly the same.

That's supposed to help correct gendered pay discrepancies. But it doesn't really work, because there are all sorts of escape hatches built in. Salary bands only cover your salary. There's lots of other ways that people get paid.

As we discussed, talent acquisition is one of them. Talent acquisition gives companies a way to pay a premium to people who have more social capital. But that's not the only way that people are rewarded unequally. There's also the sign-on bonus. The sign-on bonus in Silicon Valley today can easily be a hundred thousand dollars. Even for somebody coming off their first job, or maybe even right out of school, it can be upward of fifty thousand dollars. And the recruiters have a lot of leeway in setting that number. Then there's your annual bonus, which is a percentage of your salary at most companies. Finally, there's your stock-based compensation.

When you take an offer at a company, you're given either stock options or grants of shares in the company. Those options or grants vest over a four-year schedule. And there's really no restriction on how high that can go. So for a lot of people, a majority of total compensation comes from stock. Salary typically tops out at around $200,000 or $250,000 at a big company. But it wouldn't be surprising to be given another $100,000 in stock grants. If you're joining a company early on, that stock, by the time you're done vesting it, could be more like a million dollars.

What about ageism in the industry? Silicon Valley tends to be very young. Does that worry you as you get older?

I don't know where all the old programmers go. They must go somewhere. It is a little worrisome. I'm in my thirties, and I feel like I have less energy. I'm an iOS developer and I haven't learned Swift.* Five years ago, definitely ten years ago, the day Swift was announced I would have become an expert on it. And I just don't have that energy now.

So it sounds like issues around equity and bias played a determining role in changing how you think about the industry.

Well, come to think of it, those are issues I've only come to understand in the past few years.

I think what really shifted my thinking about my success was observing that most of the startups that are getting crazy amounts of venture capital aren't solving interesting problems. There is a lot of money going into squeezing more ad dollars out of users, and getting more attention and eyeballs. Yo is a good example.† My app wasn't much dumber than Yo. And they got millions of dollars of funding.

I also felt like people were becoming founders and investors not because they wanted to solve problems that would help humanity but because they wanted to be in the Silicon Valley scene. They wanted the cultural cachet. They wanted to go to the parties.

---

* Swift is a programming language developed by Apple for its operating systems, including iOS.

† Yo is a mobile app initially released in 2014. At first, the app's only feature was the ability to send the word "Yo" to your friends. Within a few months of launching, Yo boasted a valuation of five to ten million dollars.

That was disillusioning to me, because I had really bought into the ideology that building a business was the best way to make the world a better place. That was something that was drilled into my head at my elite college. I had completely bought into it.

But over the years, as I saw what products were being funded and built, I felt disappointed. It changed how I thought about my own success. I wasn't actually solving problems—I was just riding a wave of ridiculous overinvestment in social apps.

So your own success started to feel more like a failure—not a personal failure, perhaps, but the failure of the industry more broadly. Recently, a number of high-level people in Silicon Valley have expressed some degree of disillusionment as well. Early Facebook investor Sean Parker, among others, seems to regret his role in building a platform he now considers psychologically damaging. How do you see this disillusionment playing out more broadly in the industry?

Get wealthy and solve the world's problems—this was the message that I absorbed early on. You couldn't do one without the other, the argument went, so don't feel bad about becoming rich. The profit motive is the only way that we can possibly solve problems at scale.

I truly believed that. And it remains a widespread belief in the industry, and in the engineering departments of elite institutions. But to move forward, I think we are going to have to challenge that belief very directly. That's why I'm skeptical of some of these new-found regrets expressed by Sean Parker and others. I don't think they're actually attacking the core notion that the profit motive is the best way to make the world a better place. They still believe they can centralize large amounts of capital in these massive corporations and pay themselves well *and* solve the world's problems. I think there are some inherent trade-offs that they're not yet acknowledging.

Sean Parker is also a billionaire. Do you see rank-and-file tech workers expressing doubts about what they're building as well?

When you're an engineer, you're constantly being told to do things that are clearly not good for the user. If you're building any kind of app or platform that makes its money from advertising, you are trying to maximize "time spent"—how long a user spends with your product. Time spent is considered a proxy for value delivered to the user, because if your product wasn't useful, the user wouldn't be using it.

Here's how it typically works. An order comes down from on high: the board says to increase revenue. What's the best way the management team knows to increase revenue? To increase time spent. So they issue the order, which gets percolated down the tree, and now everyone is working on increasing time spent. This means making the product more addictive, more absorbing, more obtrusive.

And it works: the user starts spending more time with the product.

But every worker knows this is bad. Every engineer and designer knows this is awful. They're not happy making these features. But they can't argue with the data. The engineer and the designer who care about the user don't want to put these features out in the world. But the data says those features are increasing time spent—which means they're good. Because more time spent means selling more advertising, which means making more money.

And so long as you're working for an advertising company, what other metric besides time spent could there be?

So long as you're working for a company, what other metric besides profit could there be? That's a similar question. You can make small surface-level improvements here and there. But you're not going to tackle the core problem until you tackle the profit motive.

The directives to increase metrics like time spent come from above, but the actual work is being done by tech workers on the ground. And they're doing this work because their performance is measured by whether or not they moved that metric and whether or not they implemented those features—even if they know they're bad for users.

But there's no way they can push back on it. They can talk about it—in their company Slack, in their public forums, at their all-hands meetings. They can express a lot of malaise about it. But they can't argue against the experiment succeeding, because you can't argue against increased profits.

You could imagine different structures of the company that might not have this problem. You could imagine a world where these companies empower rank-and-file workers to make certain decisions themselves, and give users a voice in those decisions. Workers and users could together decide what metrics to optimize for, and what kind of technology they want to build.

Have you seen this begin to happen in your own workplace, or in the workplaces of friends? What might it look like concretely to give workers and users a say in how products are designed and implemented?

I've started to see some changes. Broadly, we tech workers are starting to find our voice in saying no. No, we won't build that weapons system at Google; no, we don't want to game metrics.* These small victories feel invigorating, but saying no isn't enough.

It's probably easier to start small. My favorite video game studio, Motion Twin, describes itself as an "anarcho-syndicalist workers' cooperative," and they have a close relationship with their community of gamers. These alter-

---

* Google had a contract with the Pentagon to help with Project Maven, an ongoing Pentagon initiative to use machine learning to analyze

native structures are possible in tech, but we're up against unbelievable amounts of venture capital that can scale for-profit ventures faster than any cooperative can.

We're starting to ask the right questions about technology and who owns it. We've tried private control. Now we're talking about worker control. There is also a lot we could do with state backing, but that has its own risks. Then there are ideas floating around like platform cooperatives, where platforms are owned and governed by a combination of their creators and their users. I think we should be trying out lots of things and seeing what works. Soon, I hope to be able to do some experiments of my own.

---

drone footage. After a monthslong campaign by workers at Google, management announced in June 2018 that it would not be renewing the Project Maven contract.

2

The Technical Writer

Silicon Valley, as you might expect, is crawling with software engineers. But writing code is only one of many jobs that make the industry run. Plenty of other white-collar labor is needed—and many of the people performing it are women.

These are the so-called nontechnical roles, and it's where Silicon Valley's stark gender divide grows even starker. Google is nearly 70 percent men; Facebook, 63 percent; Apple, 67 percent. When it comes to the "technical" part of the workforce, however, the numbers get even worse: 77 percent men at all three companies. This imbalance partly accounts for the industry's gender pay gap, because people who are seen as less technical tend to be valued less. But what does "technical" even mean? Is a customer support associate who patiently helps customers debug their code really not technical?

We spoke to a technical writer about what it's like to be a woman in tech perceived to be less technical, despite having the word "technical" in her title. She spoke about navigating the industry's gender politics, why she almost left as a result, and how she found a way to stay.

✲

How did you get into tech?
In college, I wanted to be an editor. I wanted to find the next big writer and nurture their career. When I graduated, I quickly realized that wasn't going to happen. Entry-level jobs in publishing are difficult to find, especially if you're not in New York.

So I started looking around for a job. I'd been working the night shift at a factory to cover my student loan payments while I was finishing school. But I needed better-paying work. Eventually I ended up applying for an entry-level technical writing job, having taken a couple of technical writing courses at college.

Had you considered the possibility of becoming a technical writer when you were in college?
No, I never saw myself going into technical writing. It was just the first job that I got. I took it because I needed to pay rent.

Tell us about that first job.
It was a financial software company, so it was a cross between tech and finance. Both are highly masculine industries that tend to have problems with women. So, as a young woman coming right out of college, I dealt with a lot of inappropriate comments.

In my interview, they had asked me some weird questions, like, "How would you react if someone was throwing paper balls at you all day?" It turns out the two men interviewing me asked that because they knew the team lead was extremely unprofessional, especially with young women. He wasn't sexually harassing them. But he didn't treat them as equals. They wanted to make sure that I would be able to stand up to him.

He definitely had problems. I remember going out to lunch with him and another person and he started rating the women that walked past us on a one-to-ten scale. I remember not saying anything because I didn't know what to say.

So this person was your boss?
Yeah. He was the one who divided up the tasks. And he gave me a lot to do—very soon after I arrived, I ended up with the lion's share of the work. I was on a team of three technical writers. The other two were men, and I probably had three times as much work as they did, although I was being paid significantly less.

What did you do?
Well, eventually our team lead left. That made things better. I moved under a different manager, and during our first performance review he took me aside and said, "I know that you do most of the work and that you're underpaid." And then he gave me a 40 percent raise.

Wow.
Yeah. It totally changed my career. I stayed there for about five years.

You said that you had taken a couple of technical writing classes in college, but presumably you also learned a lot in that first job. What did you learn? What is technical writing?

I usually compare it to IKEA. When you buy something from IKEA, the only way you know how to put it together is by looking at the instruction manual. It's the glue that holds everything together.

There are the people who build a product—engineers, designers, and so on. Then there are the people who explain how to use the product. That's us.

Could you give us an example?

My first company made financial trading software. And we needed to explain to our customers what the requirements were for installing that software and getting it to run properly.

When I got there, we had a thirty-two-page document explaining all this. It was unusable. Customers were very confused about what they needed to do. So I turned it into a two-pager. That was my first moment of realizing, "Oh, technical writing really is necessary. I can provide real value."

How well do engineers and executives understand that value?

It's highly dependent on the kind of engineer or executive you're working with. The stereotypical dynamic is that you're not valued. They don't really understand what you're doing in the room. They talk over you or talk down to you because writing is seen as a soft skill. We're seen as humanities people. Even though technical writers are some of the only people who actually have "technical" in their role name, we're not seen as technical. People assume we don't know what we're talking about.

Presumably, this is also a highly gendered dynamic.
A lot of technical writers are women. At my current job, my whole team is women. And all women in tech deal with the perception that we're nontechnical. Which means we are paid less. You see this particularly with equity. In tech, your equity generally depends on how technical you are perceived to be.

With technical writing in particular, perhaps some people see it as less valuable because writing is something that they do all the time, even if it's just writing emails.
It's a way to devalue the craft. It's like saying that product designers are just there to make things look pretty.

Technical writing is actually probably only about 10 percent writing. It's a small portion of the job. Most of your time is spent on research, information architecture, content strategy—all these related disciplines. It's not about typing words on a screen and publishing them somewhere. It's about telling the right story to your users so they know how to use the product.

And some products are harder to use than others.
Sometimes people forget that not all software looks like email. There's a lot of software that's actually pretty complex. A lot can go wrong. And the stakes are high when it does. If users do the wrong thing when using a big piece of enterprise software, for example, that company could lose millions of dollars.

It seems strange that certain people would find it hard to see the value in technical writing, when the success of a product so clearly depends on it. The product is not usable if users can't use it.
Absolutely. And I have found, especially in the last few years, that a lot of people don't conform to the above stereotype. They see the value in what we do. It's nice to work with folks like that.

Source of Truth

After five years at that first company, you had become an experienced technical writer. What happened next?
I had a couple more jobs before I landed what I thought was my dream position. I would be the first technical writer at a small company. I was really excited.

It turned out to be a strange place. They were focused on creating a fun company that people wanted to work at—Ping-Pong tables, that startup feel—but without any real substance behind it. They just didn't know what they were doing. I was one of the oldest people working there and I was twenty-nine.

The two cofounders told me they didn't want any external documentation. They wanted *internal* documentation. And they wanted me to document the product not as it actually existed, but as they had originally envisioned it.

The problem is that the two cofounders had each envisioned it differently. So I would sit in a room with them and listen to them argue. "No, we meant for it to look like this!" "No, we wanted it to happen this way!" It was a mess.

You said that technical writing is the art of explaining to the user how to use the product. But you can't do that if you're not allowed to be honest with the user about what the product is.

Documentation is the source of truth. It's not marketing. It's not sales.

You're there to be honest with the user. You have to be willing to talk about the limitations, the bugs. You have to be willing to talk about the behaviors that will break everything. It's important because if users don't trust your product, they're not going to use your product. Technical documentation is the place where you build that trust.

There's a push and pull sometimes between the various groups. When I talk to folks in marketing, they're looking at it from the perspective of how to sell the product. When they see a piece of documentation that describes the product less positively, they don't understand why it needs to be said that way. So we have a conversation, and try to come to a middle ground where we both feel comfortable. Then, once they're not paying attention anymore, I sneak back in the stuff that users really need to know.

At this particular company, where the cofounders couldn't agree on what the product was, how did you do your job?

Despite the issues I mentioned, I found a way to move forward. I started writing internal documentation. I created a style guide and I laid the foundations for having technical content more widely shared within the company. I was working well with the developers.

My manager and I had a great working relationship. I had a good performance review. Everything was roses. Then I got pregnant with my second child and I started to take some time off. Just mornings here and there when I woke up and thought, I can't do it. I'm going to throw up—I can't go into work. At the time, I had a two-hour commute each way.

I hadn't told my company that I was pregnant yet, because conventional wisdom says to wait till you get to that twelve-week mark when things feel safer. When I reached that point, I had a conversation with HR. The company was so small that they didn't have a formal HR department, just a guy who was filling that role. He had no official training, but he was a nice guy. So I pulled him aside and asked about maternity leave. There was no policy in the handbook, because I was the first person at the company who had ever been pregnant.

What did he say?
He said he would talk to the cofounders and get back to me. That sounded good to me. I figured the maternity leave wouldn't be great, but it would be something.

Soon after, on the day I was planning to announce my pregnancy to the rest of the company, one of the cofounders pulled me into a conference room. He told me that things weren't working out so they were going to eliminate my role.

What?
He also said that because I was technically negative in my time off—those days when I was too sick or tired from pregnancy to come into work—I owed the company five days' pay. Normally, it doesn't matter if you're negative: you just keep accruing days and it evens out. He told me he wouldn't make me pay them back for those days, but in exchange, I wouldn't be getting any severance.

I was very upset. I told him I was about to announce that I was pregnant. He said he didn't know.

Did you believe him?
I'll never know if he knew. But I'm pretty sure he did. There is no smoking gun I can point to. But my guess is that the HR guy told him. He probably figured it wasn't worth it to pay for maternity leave, so it'd be easier just

to get rid of me. And it wasn't illegal, because they eliminated the role, not the person.

Did you talk to a lawyer?

No. People told me I should have, but I just couldn't. I was so upset at the time, I signed the paperwork and went home sobbing. I was tired. I was pregnant.

I also didn't want to rock the boat. Because the worry when you're a woman in tech is that if you raise your voice, you'll get branded as a troublemaker. Tech is actually kind of a small industry. You don't want to be the woman who's not easy to work with. I was so scared at that moment that I didn't do the right thing.

False Choices

Did you start looking for another job right away?

I did. But it's hard to find a job when you're pregnant. It was my second pregnancy and I was already showing. Then I had the kid, which didn't make it any easier. Trying to find a job with a newborn is impossible.

My husband was working, which meant we were on his health care. But his salary wasn't enough to pay all of our bills. So I had to bring money in one way or another. Fortunately, I found contract work. Contract work has saved me time and time again.

I would take care of my kids during the day. Then I would put them to bed and start working. I was really doing two jobs at once.

What were your days typically like?

I probably averaged about four hours of sleep a night. I would wake up around 5:30 a.m. and go to bed around 1:00 a.m. I would take naps with my kids in the afternoon. That was how I got through. I would force my toddler to take a nap when the baby did. Then I would take a nap with them.

It was a delicate dance. I was very tired for about two years.

That sounds really hard.

It wasn't all bad. Contract jobs typically pay well, so I was able to pay off a lot of things, including my student loans. That was great. But I was out of full-time work for almost two years, which was terrifying.

How did you find your way back to full-time work?

There was a long period where I didn't think I would. I was just done. I didn't want to work in tech anymore. I wanted to go a completely different route. I was kicking myself for taking that first technical writing job, thinking, What did I get myself into?

What changed your mind?

I used to ask my daughter, "What do you want to be when you grow up?" And when I was working full-time, she said, "I want to be a writer, like you!" Or, "I want to be an artist, like Dad!" He's a designer.

Then, after I had been home for a while, her answer began to change. Even though I was still doing contract work, she didn't really understand that. She just knew I was at home. So she started saying, "I want to be a mommy, like you."

Now, there's nothing wrong with being a full-time parent. It's a super admirable thing to do. But, personally, it broke my heart to hear my daughter say that. I didn't want to be instilling that idea. So in that moment, I decided that I was going to find my way back to tech. I was going to find a place to work that wouldn't treat me in the way that I had been treated.

Where did you start?

I focused on remote jobs. I figured that people who trust their employees to work from home will treat them like adults.

And eventually I landed at a wonderful place. Most of the people who work there are remote. I've been there almost four years. I've been promoted three times within that time period, and I'm leading the team now.

Tell us more about why working remotely is so important to you.

Being able to work remotely is the entire reason that I've been able to keep a full-time job while having two small children.

There's a million doctor's appointments and school functions. They don't actually take that much time. But if you're working on-site, you just can't do them all. You can't take your kid to that twenty-minute doctor's appointment that they need to get antibiotics. You can't show up to the thirty-minute classroom party where the parents just stand in the corner.

So being able to work remotely has really enabled me to be there as a parent and not give up those things that matter to me, while still being able to contribute professionally in a meaningful way. When you work remotely, you don't have to feel guilty about asking your boss if you can work from home one day or leave early another day.

For instance, at one of my former full-time positions, I had wanted to take my kids trick-or-treating on Halloween. The trick-or-treating starts in my neighborhood at 7:00 p.m. I had a two-hour commute, so I had to leave work at 3:00 p.m. to get home with enough time to put my kids into their costumes. My boss told me I was allowed to leave early, but that I would have to come in early the next day. So the following morning I was in the office at 5:00 a.m. I turned the lights on that day, just so I could take my kids trick-or-treating.

I shouldn't have to choose between my kids and my work. Working remotely means I don't have to.

If working remotely is not an option, I imagine that many women will just opt out of tech entirely for the reasons you're describing. So this also has major consequences for gender inequality within the tech industry.

Exactly. There are a ton of women who had to leave tech when they had kids. How do we support women who are trying to come back into the industry when their kids are a little older and they're ready to make that transition? What resources can we provide?

It's frustrating to have to face this problem, because it's very specific to women. In general, women are still expected to fill certain roles in the home and be a parent in a way that men aren't.

I'd imagine these types of gendered exclusions happen early in the hiring process. Like if someone has gaps in their résumé because they were raising a kid, it's counted against them.

Yes. Not just from the perspective of whether they'll get the job, but also how much they should be paid. Because people assume that if you're out of the industry for a few months, you're behind on things. There's a belief that the technology is moving so fast that if you fail to keep up with it even for a moment, you'll no longer have the relevant qualifications. Women already face a huge pay gap in tech, and this sort of thing just exacerbates the problem.

My first boss at my first job, the one I was telling you about, once made a comment along these lines that I will never forget. He said that women *should* be paid less when they take time off to have a baby. Because if they're out of the workforce for a month or two, they'll be less valuable when they come back. Therefore their pay should be docked.

That's a surprisingly pervasive attitude among men

in tech. They think women who are taking maternity leave are doing it for fun or something. They think we're having a vacation. So why should we make as much money as men?

The Conversations Are Louder

In addition to having more remote-friendly policies, what are the other kinds of things you think tech companies could do to reduce gender inequality?
Put in place better programs to train their managers. Managers have an enormous amount of power. As I've moved into a leadership role myself, I see how little training there is. I hire people, I promote people, I give them raises, I sponsor them, I coach them—and I do all of this with no real training. There's nothing preventing me from imparting my own biases. And that's a terrifying thing to see from the inside.

It seems like one common career path in tech is that if you do well as an individual contributor, you move into management. But just because someone is a good software engineer doesn't mean they'll be a good manager.
Yeah, it's a totally different set of skills. But there isn't much agreement on what those skills even are. For most people, it's a complete black box.

When I moved into a leadership role, I joined Slack

communities where managers give one another advice. Some of the things they say are pretty wild. The women and nonbinary folks had to create another private channel just for us, where we talk about how we can influence the men to not be shitty.

So, yes, we need better criteria for who we promote into management and better training to remove people's biases, or at least be aware of them. We need to be more intentional about the kind of environment we're trying to create, and understand the roles that individual managers play in creating that environment.

Are managers in tech especially powerful? Is there something about the greater informality of tech workplaces and their "flatter" organizational hierarchies that tends to leave more decisions to managerial discretion?

Let's say you have salary ranges for the different levels of a particular role. That's a way to help standardize pay and reduce gender disparities. But those ranges can be as big as a hundred thousand dollars. And it's up to the manager to place a new hire within that range.

So, all the time, I see men who are hired in at higher rates than women with the same amount of experience. Again, it all comes down to the individual manager. Maybe that manager saw something that makes them see the woman as a little less technical. Maybe that woman wasn't at a well-known company. So they bring her in lower because they have these biases against things that women have no control over, and which does not actually speak to the value they will bring to the organization.

In recent years, we've seen a bigger public conversation about gender inequality in tech. There have also been actions by tech workers against gender inequality that have received media attention, such as the Google walkout in November 2018.* What's it like to have these conversations grow?

These conversations have been happening in back channels for a long time. Not just around women, but around any minority group in tech. If they're not happening in back channels, they're happening within people's heads. We know what's going on. We know the situation.

Now there's this heightened scrutiny. People are calling out things for being unjust, and that's great. But the heightened scrutiny is not necessarily productive. The media, for example, can be exhausting. There were articles written about my company a couple of years ago that I found really frustrating.

Why?

Because we were having these conversations among trusted back-channel groups internally. Then all of a sudden it

---

* On November 1, 2018, twenty thousand Googlers, both full-time employees and contract workers, walked out from some fifty offices around the world. They were protesting gender discrimination and sexual harassment at the company, angered in particular by the disclosure that Andy Rubin, the creator of Android, had received a ninety-million-dollar exit package amid a sexual harassment investigation.

became a public issue and the narrative was taken away from us. The media makes you out to be victims. You become part of a bigger story about women being mistreated in tech. It's really tiring after a while.

It sounds like what you find tiring about the media attention is being made into the object, not the subject, of the story. That you're being presented as the victim, and not as someone with autonomy and agency.

Yes, that's exactly it.

I mean, just look at the entire situation with James Damore.* The story was all about him. It was all about his beliefs and his backstory. He was the subject. He got to have all the autonomy and the agency.

The Damore thing is also interesting because it demonstrates how, as the conversations around diversity become bigger and more visible, people who are not from underrepresented groups start to join them. You see a lot of new voices coming in who don't really have the context to participate constructively. They don't really understand the situation, but they feel entitled to offer their opinions. So spaces that were previously smaller and more trusted are now being expanded, and it's usually not for the better.

You can no longer use those spaces to vent. Instead,

---

* James Damore was a Google engineer. In July 2017, he published an internal memo that criticized Google's diversity policies and claimed that the overrepresentation of men in tech was partly due to innate biological differences that made women less suitable for certain kinds of work. The next month, he was fired.

you're being asked to defend your existence within tech on a larger stage. So a lot of women just back out of the conversation completely, because they don't want to be put in the position of being the voice of all women.

So the conversations are louder. There are more people involved. But that doesn't necessarily make them better.

3

The Cook

The people who populate tech aren't just software engineers, technical writers, and other white-collar workers. They're also the security guards, shuttle drivers, janitors, and cafeteria staff who work on office campuses across Silicon Valley. Their labor is often invisible but completely indispensable: if they don't do their job, nobody else can do theirs.

Tech's blue-collar workers are overwhelmingly people of color, and many are immigrants. Despite working in one of the world's most profitable industries, they earn very low wages: a 2016 study found that they make on average about twenty thousand dollars a year, less than the median annual rent in Santa Clara County, which encompasses Silicon Valley. In response to this punishing math, many of these workers have unionized in recent years, winning higher wages and better benefits. But even with a union, life is hard—long hours, long commutes, and the manifold hardships and indignities that come with sitting in the shadow of Silicon Valley's wealth.

We spoke to a cook at a major tech company who knows this life well. This is someone with deep roots in the Bay Area, with vivid memories of the first dot-com boom and firsthand experience of the industry's local imprint. We talked about what it's like to cook food in tech, what it's like to organize a union in tech, and what the future might hold for the region.

✷

Where did you grow up?
I grew up in West Oakland, California, with my mom and dad, brothers and sisters. It was fun. It was hard. It was poor. We had a Texas Instruments calculator and used to play a game called *Lode Runner* on it. That's the most tech we ever had. But I had good family, good friends. Oakland was the best place ever to grow up.

At some point, I started making really, really, really, really, really poor decisions—the kind of decisions that your parents tell you not to make. This led to discipline by my father. I got kicked out of the house when I was fifteen or sixteen. I started doing little side jobs, and staying with friends. Ultimately, I ended up having a son. That's when I realized I had to start doing things super different. So I started working in the irrigation industry, which was a hot industry back then.

When was that?
That was right around when CNN ran a special called *Silicon Valley: The New Gold Rush* [1999]. That's when I started working in irrigation. It was like *boom*—you could see it. All around this area: Atherton, Menlo Park, Palo Alto, Mountain View, San Jose. Irrigation was good business because everybody was having money around here. You

can tell the economy's doing good when people are taking care of their yards. It was a beautiful time. Irrigation was hard work, but it paid well.

Then around 2008, the irrigation business started going bad. That's when we had the housing crash. People couldn't afford to get their houses done. In fact, they could barely afford to keep their houses—and a lot of people had bought their houses on fake-ass Wells Fargo bank loans and whatnot. That just, like, shook up the whole world. Suddenly, everybody was vulnerable. Even the irrigation company I was working for wasn't able to keep up their payments.

So I ended up going to culinary school. It was my dad's idea, before he passed away. He knew I liked to cook. Me and him had butted heads just my whole upbringing—I never wanted to do anything he felt like I should do. But I ended up going to culinary school. Which was bullshit—I swear that culinary school is the biggest bullshit ever.

Why's that?
Because they charge you so much, and you don't even get the job they tell you that you're gonna get. It *does* teach you how to cook. I'll give them that: if you go to culinary school, you will learn how to cook. I did. I thought I knew how to cook, but I didn't know shit. When I got out, I went to work for one of the biggest tech companies in the area, as a prep cook making twelve dollars an hour. That was around 2010 or 2011, I think.

Were you hired directly by the company?

No. As cooks, we're contract workers. We're not direct employees of those companies. We have to go through a staffing agency. A lot of people I went to culinary school with went through those agencies, too.

What was your first impression of tech? What was it like working for that company?

It was . . . hella wack. The people at that company . . . they were different. They really weren't that cool. At the time, the tech workers thought they were the shit. They were getting all the perks and bonuses. They were at a fresh-ass company that was about to take over everything, and they knew it. I ain't gonna be mad at them, but they were snobby as hell. You saw the Benzes, the Lamborghinis, the Porsches, the Ferraris, the Bentleys popping all up in the parking lot.

Some people got more sense now. Back then they were a little different. A lot of people forgot where they came from when they got some money, I guess.

How long did you stay at that company?

I was there for a couple years. My coworkers were good people. The chef I worked for, he taught me a lot. But after a couple years, I left and went to a restaurant. I like working in restaurants, but they don't pay. You're making really good food for really good people, and it's a fun atmosphere. But you're busting your ass doing a lot of work, and it doesn't pay. After the restaurant, I went to a catering company. That was cool, too. But once again, it didn't pay enough.

That's why I left. I was like, I need health care. I got a son. He's active. He's an athlete. If I don't have health care, with the price of health care what it is, I couldn't even afford a single Tylenol in the ambulance. You don't really have a choice: you've got to go back over there and work for the tech companies. It's hard for restaurants and catering companies to keep cooks, because they can't pay the money that the tech companies can pay. These companies can drop a new building or a new campus anywhere, and they're gonna need people to come in there and cook. So I started working for a different big tech company, which is where I still work.

It had been a few years since you last worked in tech by the time you went back. Had the mood changed? Did tech feel different?

Yeah, it did. The climate was different. At my current company, the tech workers are hella cool. They just chilling and getting their money, trying to have a good time. They work a lot. They bust their ass.

Could you walk us through a normal day?

I get up early in the morning, usually at 5:00 a.m., and I get to work by 6:00 a.m. We prepare food. Then we take a break. Then we prepare more food. The service comes, and we serve the food. Then we clean up and get out at 3:00 p.m.

But everybody's gotta have two jobs. Myself, I just started a new part-time gig. Most of my coworkers, when they get out at 3:00 p.m., they go to another job and work another shift. With the way traffic is, they have to go straight there. They have to be at their second job at 4:00 or 5:00 p.m. to get that next eight hours in, so they can at least be home before midnight. Many of them live so far out: they've got to go drive all the way home to East San Jose or Gilroy or Morgan Hill. I heard some people are even coming from Vallejo. You know how far that is from here? With traffic, that's like a two-hour trip.

So that's the typical day for most people. Start at 6:00 a.m., get home by midnight. They're busting their ass. They're really busting their ass. But you have to. Especially if you got kids.

Are a lot of the people you work with from the Bay Area originally?
A lot of people did grow up here. But they're getting forced out. They're moving further and further out. A lot of them are having to set down new roots when they still have their old roots here.

As someone who grew up here, you must've seen a lot of change over the years.
Oh, yes, a lot of change. I went to my mother's neighborhood in West Oakland recently, where I grew up. That neighborhood was notorious. It had a lot of negative activity. Now they have houses there going for a

million plus. Like, *nice* houses. They put some work in them.

But the changes that were made, I don't think they were the best ones for the people. Low-income cities like East Palo Alto could've invested in low-income housing instead of bringing in IKEA and Home Depot. Why we got a fucking PGA golf store in the middle of the hood? I mean, I get it: the rich cities around us need a place to come shop. But that all used to be housing. So you take the housing away, and now you put the problem on the people.

If you ride down El Camino you see nothing but hotels. Hotels, but no housing. They're building those hotels for the tech industry, so all these people can come in and do big business here. But they ain't let us—the people that's living here—get no part of the big business. That's wack.

A Really Good Feeling

I know you were active in organizing a union in your workplace. How did you start getting involved in that?
Some homies that I work with pulled me aside and said, "We want to unionize." And then they introduced me to the people from the union. They wanted to make power moves. They wanted to give the workers the power to actually have a voice and make some changes. I thought it

made sense. So I started going to some meetings with my coworkers.

When and where would you meet?
We met at people's houses. Or after work we'd chop it up in the parking lot for a minute. We'd go have a beer or pizza or something like that.

It was cool. We heard each other's stories. We heard about how hard it is for each of us to get by and raise a family. And once you get to know your coworkers, you start seeing things a lot differently. You want to help them out. You want to make it fair.

As you started talking to your coworkers about organizing a union, did you have any challenging conversations? How did you try to convince people to support the effort?
It was hard. People are afraid they'll lose their job. And they got a family. That's a real-life situation. How do you get over it? The union people pump you up. They have you feeling juice like, "Yeah, if he gets fired I'm gonna walk off the job with him! They can't fire us all!"

There's a movie called *Which Way Is Up?* with Richard Pryor. Go back and watch that movie and you'll see exactly how the whole system works. Because you don't always know which way is up. It's hard. People got shit on the line. They got families. But it's needed. So you've got to keep pushing.

You talk to one person, and the next person talks to

somebody else they trust. And so on, until you have a nice little core. And of course you've got to have some clowns like me, who ain't got no sense so they talk loud and talk hella shit and get everybody fired up.

Were you scared? Excited? Both? How did it all feel?
It's a really good feeling. When people actually realize that they are worth more, it's nice.

But once we went public with the union, and started negotiating our contract, it was difficult. That process was new for me. I had never sat down at a negotiating table before or read a contract.

How long did negotiations take?
A long time. It was painstaking.

What were the main things you were negotiating over?
For different people it was different things. But for me . . . I like to talk shit. I like to run my mouth. So I wanted the chance to just be like, "Yeah, man, fuck y'all!" Also, I needed a raise. I needed the benefits.

But it's hard, because you can't go on in there and ask for everything. You want to act like you can. You want to act hella hard-core and whatnot. But then management responds, and you start seeing your people fall back. So you have to make choices about which demands are more important.

It caused a bit of bickering, of course. "We should get this much." "Nah, we should get this much." "This is more important than that." "No, we need this." People disagree. Then at the next meeting, some people aren't there because they can't get what they want. You can't please everybody.

You weren't negotiating directly with the tech company, because you're contractors. But obviously the tech company has a lot of influence over the contracting company. During the negotiations, did you encounter full-time tech workers who were supportive of your unionization effort?
Yes. They were a big help. I think they're really cool people. Like, weird cool. Like, computer techie hacker cool. They came through and stood up and put the word out. They showed up at meetings and some of them even came to negotiations. They just went above and beyond. Hella cool-ass people.

The Tech Workers Coalition* is forming these groups now that reach out and understand that everybody working for a tech company should be part of that company, in one sense or another. You see, these companies don't want to hire the help themselves. They'd rather hire the help to get the help, so to speak. Above all, they don't want to be responsible for the help.

Service workers like us are at the bottom of the list.

---

* Tech Workers Coalition is an organization of tech workers that has been active in organizing efforts throughout the industry.

And since we're at the bottom, we didn't have any say. They could just treat us however.

Did that change after you unionized? I know that you negotiated for better wages and better benefits, but did the workplace *feel* different after you formed a union? In terms of how you were treated?

It definitely felt different. Even before we got our contract, when management first found out we were organizing, it changed the workplace. In our kitchens, the chefs are the bosses and the cooks are the workers. Right away, the chefs started showing a little more class. They started treating us nicer. Before, most of them treated us like peasants. Honestly. Most of the time they didn't talk to us. They were just there to discipline us and keep us in line. But when they found out we were going to organize, *their* bosses were like, "Hey, y'all better get y'all shit together. Because we don't need this kind of tension."

Who are the chefs? Did they used to be cooks? Or do they come in as supervisors?

Just like any other company, some of them get hired into that position and some of them come in as a cook and work their way up—the ones who kiss ass.

You ever watch *The Office*? That's pretty much how every workplace is. It's definitely like that in the kitchen. You got your boss that's the idiot. Then you got the one dude who just don't give a fuck. Then you got your nice normal people. Then you got all the ass-kissers—there's a bunch of wannabe Dwights running around. They know what you're going through because they went through it, but once they get their assistant regional manager title, they just start going hard-core on you.

But when our organizing went public, and that tone shift happened, it was nice. My coworkers and I laughed about it, actually: "He just asked me how my day was!" "He just said, 'Thank you'!" Simple shit like that. They started treating us like people. That was a good feeling. That was a really, really good feeling.

Happy Bill Gates Day!

Now that you've won your union, what's next?
You gotta keep organizing *after* you organize. That's the most crucial part. It was hard work getting the union, but it's even harder work keeping it.

When we first ratified our contract, a lot of people were happy: "Cool, I got a raise!" But then when they actually got that first raise, and it ain't really what they thought, then they're like, "Man, y'all could've got more." Like, what? You weren't even coming to the meetings!

It's hard. We started out with a small group of organizers. Then we became a big group—and if you stay big like that, you can really run shit. They're really going to feel it.

Look at the Oakland teachers.* When they went on

---

* On February 21, 2019, Oakland teachers went on strike. The strike lasted for seven days, and forced school officials to make major concessions after more than eighteen months of failed negotiations.

strike, they shut shit down. We don't have the power to do that yet. Maybe one day. But again, it's hard to keep people organized. Especially now, as our company grows, we have new cooks coming in who don't know the struggles that we had to go through. And in general, people don't know much about unions.

Unions used to be a big deal back in the day. They used to be so tough, so fierce, so hard-core. And I get it. I understand why unions were so big. Because they honestly do give you that sense of power if you really listen to the message.

I heard a rumor that some of the white-collar tech workers were thinking about unionizing.

That's right.
That's crazy to me. But it shows you how wack it is out there. A lot of tech workers are like us to a certain extent.

I knew a tech worker who said she was a contractor like me.* I didn't even know that they had tech workers as contractors at those companies. So they feel us. They feel the pain. As I said earlier, the company would rather hire the help to get the help. It's easier. They don't want that liability and they don't want to pay. Because if you're a contractor, you don't get those good benefits. You don't

---

* While tech companies have long used contractors for blue-collar service roles such as cooks, security guards, and shuttle bus drivers, they increasingly employ contractors for white-collar office roles as well, from programming to testing to recruiting.

get those perks. It's kind of fucked-up. So now a lot of the tech workers, they're feeling like us. And they can't afford the houses, either, because they're getting better money than us, but they're not really getting enough.

You work in tech, but how do you use tech in your own life? What do you think of social media, for instance?
I think it's a little invasive. You know, I'm old-school. I don't like people in my business. And I don't care if your daughter is thirteen months and just started walking. That's none of my business. I really could care less. You don't have to post that on there. That's normal to me. I went through that. I saw my son walking when he was ten months.

My son is a clown at times. He's a teenager now, and teenagers today are more influenced by social media than they are by their parents. A person can get a million views or likes or whatnot for doing something goofy and then become famous in less than a year. My son will see that and think it could be him. But if things don't work out, now his ass is in trouble, because he did some stupid shit.

When I was a teenager, we didn't have dating sites. We didn't have Snapchat and Instagram. I had a pager! I used to have to page chicks "143"—I love you, that goofy shit. Nowadays, these kids are dealing with a whole other beast.

I took his phone away recently. And he's changing a little bit every day. He actually threw his stuff in the garbage yesterday. I was like, Wow, this is amazing. It's working already! He's actually putting shit in the garbage like he's supposed to!

Where do you think Silicon Valley will go next? You've seen a huge amount of change since the 1990s. What will the next couple of decades look like?

You ever see *Demolition Man*, that movie with Sylvester Stallone and Wesley Snipes? Where Snipes has blond hair?

Yeah.

That could be where we're going.

Damn.

The near future is gonna be hard. Really hard. We're going to make some changes, with the help of the organizers and the unions and all of the other people that are pushing to make a change. But I worry that it's too little, too late. I worry that it's not going to be enough to actually help the people that need to be helped now.

A lot of people are leaving the Bay. A lot of people are leaving California. They're moving to places where the cost of living isn't as high, places where you can afford a house and raise a family. That's the dream, right? You got a house, two kids, a car, and a soccer van, and you're able to take your kids to the movies. But those other places are gonna turn into here if they make the same mistakes we made: not organizing early, not getting the communities involved early.

They're having a celebration near here in a park for Cinco de Mayo. If it gets worse, that's not going to be there. That's going to be some tech holiday. It might be Bill Gates Day instead of Cinco de Mayo if things get out of hand.

4

The Engineer

Google occupies a special spot in the firmament of Silicon Valley.* It's not only one of the region's most successful companies—it also defines a cultural ideal. Silicon Valley presents itself as a playground for weird geniuses, as a place where creativity, commerce, and a little bit of counterculture fuse to form a new synthesis capable of generating extraordinary wealth. Few companies appear to embody this synthesis better than Google.

Yet over the years, Google has changed. And its transformations have paralleled the broader shifts of the region as a whole, as a generation of companies that saw themselves as eccentric underdogs evolved into corporate leviathans. At Google, this dissonance was especially intensely felt. It became a source of internal tensions, which in turn helped make the company a hot spot for white-collar worker organizing.

There is no better vantage point than Google to observe how Silicon Valley has changed in recent years. We talked to an engineer who spent nine years at the company, and experienced many of these changes firsthand. What happens when Silicon Valley's golden child grows

---

* Since a corporate restructuring in 2015, Google's parent company is called Alphabet, and Google is technically a subsidiary.

up? What does it look like for a company to have a mid-life crisis?

How did you start using computers?
I didn't really have a computer growing up. Then, when I was in high school, my parents bought one for their business. You could use the modem to dial into the BBS [bulletin board system] of the local public library, and connect to the internet from there. One of the first things that I remember thinking was, Oh, the internet is really cool!

It was around that time that I started programming. The library had a book about Perl.* So I taught myself Perl, and soon I was making websites for local businesses. That was my first tech job, I guess.

Did you go on to study computer science in college?
Yeah, I went to college in 1999. At the time, the dot-com boom was going strong. There was a lot of optimism in my undergrad class. The computer science major was bigger than it had been in previous years.

I definitely felt behind my peers. I had always been at the top of my class in math and science, but I didn't have a whole lot of programming experience. The homework was hard.

When you're first learning programming and some-

---

* Perl is a programming language that was once widely used on the web.

going to unfold in the next ten years involves companies like SoFi, or Earnest, or pretty much any company whose shtick is, "We're using big data technology and machine learning to do better credit score assessments."*

I actually think this is going to be a huge point of contention moving forward. I talked to a guy who used to work for one of these companies. Not one of the ones I mentioned, a different one. And one of their shticks was, "Oh, we're going to use social media data to figure out if you're a great credit risk or not." And people are like, "Oh, are they going to look at my Facebook posts to see whether I've been drinking out late on a Saturday night? Is that going to affect my credit score?"

And I can tell you exactly what happened, and why they actually killed that. It's because with your social media profile, they know your name, they know the names of your friends, and they can tell if you're black or not. They can tell how wealthy you are, they can tell if you're a credit risk. That's the shtick.

And my consistent point of view is that any of these companies should be presumed to be incredibly racist unless presenting you with mountains of evidence otherwise. Anybody that says, "We're an AI company that's making smarter loans": racist. Absolutely, 100 percent.

I was actually floored, during a recent Super Bowl, when I saw this SoFi ad that said, "We discriminate." I

---

* SoFi and Earnest are online lenders that offer personal loans, student loan refinancing, and other services.

thing goes wrong, you don't really know how to tell *where* it's going wrong or *why*. It's an intuition you have to develop over time. You learn where to look or what to push on to figure out why this particular piece of code isn't working the way you expected it to work. And, even for experienced programmers, you never know how long that process is going to take. Sometimes you figure it out in a few minutes, sometimes it's a few hours. Sometimes you never figure it out, and you have to start over from scratch.

What happened after you graduated college?
As I mentioned, I started college in 1999, during the dot-com boom. By the time I graduated in 2003, the bubble had popped. Given what I was hearing about the job market, I decided to go to grad school.

Did you want to become an academic?
I wasn't sure. The actual experience of being a Ph.D. student was definitely hard for me. I felt again like, Oh my God, these other people are so much smarter than me.

When it came time to identify a research topic and write a thesis proposal, I really struggled. I think that was the hardest part of the whole process. I didn't have a lot of academics among my family or friends. I didn't know where to start. By the time I got through the thesis proposal, I was drained. The whole thing had left me feeling pretty burned-out—maybe about as burned-out as I've ever been.

My adviser had a very large stable of grad students. One summer, she didn't have funding for all of us, so I ended up working with a different professor on a research project that eventually became a startup: something called reCAPTCHA.

Tell us about that.

Anybody who's been around the internet for long enough has seen a CAPTCHA. These days, it's the little thing that pops up with a checkbox that says "I am not a robot." And sometimes it asks you to prove it by clicking images that have a taxi or a traffic light or whatever.

The professor I was working for invented the original CAPTCHA for Yahoo. Back in the day, Yahoo had a bunch of people signing up for free email accounts and then using them to send spam. The CAPTCHA was supposed to put a check on that.

The idea was that you'd display this distorted text and tell the user to type it. A computer could generate these tests very easily and know what the right answer was. But at the time it was hard for computers to *read* the distorted text. So the CAPTCHA prevented people from writing programs to automatically create a hundred thousand Yahoo email accounts for sending spam.

CAPTCHAs started to get used everywhere on the web. At some point we did the math and figured out, "Wow, people are filling in millions, maybe *billions* of these a day. They are collectively wasting a huge chunk of time typing in these obnoxious characters. Why don't we try to do some good for the world and use CAPTCHAs to digitize books?"

How?
It's the same idea as the original CAPTCHA. But instead of displaying random words, you're displaying words from old books or newspapers or magazines that optical character recognition software has trouble reading. So we get humans to read the words and tell us what they are.

We would display two words. One was a word that we actually knew. The other word was taken from a scanned book, and maybe we had some guesses. We would use the word we knew to confirm that the person was actually a human. Then, assuming that they passed the first word, we would count their answer for the other word as a vote for the correct spelling of that word.

If they happened to agree with the optical character recognition software, then, great—it was probably right. If they disagreed, then maybe you send the word out to a couple more people and try to get some agreement on what the word is.

Where would you get the scanned books or newspapers or magazines?
Well, our idea was that there must be places that have old works that they want to digitize. We could partner with them. And that became the business model. It started out as an academic research project but, by the end of that

summer—this was 2007—we had decided to make it into an actual company.

We ended up getting a contract with *The New York Times*. We started digitizing old years of the paper that were in the public domain. So we started with 1922 or 1923 and then kept going backward. We went in reverse chronological order because obviously the older scans were harder to read.

That was a really fun project to work on. We were a small team, maybe six people, and we never had an office. It felt like being at another university research lab.

Then, in 2009, we found out that Google was considering acquiring us.

Into the Mothership

Why did Google want reCAPTCHA?

They wanted to use it to digitize Google Books.

At that point, Google had been scanning books in the public domain from libraries for many years. And, it wasn't announced publicly yet, but Google was getting into the e-book business.

They wanted an e-book service that could compete with the Amazon Kindle. And part of their plan for doing that was to say, "Hey, we can offer higher-quality versions of all these old public domain books than what Amazon has."

At the time, Amazon was claiming to have four hundred

thousand e-books. Three hundred thousand of those were public domain books that had been scanned by somebody and gone through one pass of optical character recognition. There would be typos or misspellings or wrong words everywhere. Not really joyful to read.

The idea was that Google could have a similar catalog of these older public domain works but that they would actually be readable. Honestly, I think it was largely a marketing thing. To be able to say, "We have five hundred thousand e-books and nobody else has five hundred thousand e-books."

So reCAPTCHA would be the weapon that Google could use to beat Amazon at e-books, by offering a way to clean up text produced by not-so-great optical recognition software.

Yeah. Google had a team, and still does, that worked on optical recognition software. The project was open-source and called Tesseract. Tesseract was closely tied to the Google Books team. We met with them during our first few weeks, and sat next to them.

Tesseract was okay, but it wasn't as good as the commercial software we had been using for reCAPTCHA, which was called ABBYY. So Google wanted reCAPTCHA to improve the text quality.

What was it like to be acquired by Google?

It was exciting. We had a lot of code that was specific to *The New York Times*. They had a particular format of articles and sections and so on. Now we were doing books, which is a very different sort of thing.

Also, the scale was completely new. At Google, we were working with *millions* of books. And we had way more access to computing power, obviously.

I'd imagine that Google had more computing resources available than your startup.
Yes, and reCAPTCHA was an old-school startup, before there was any of this cloud stuff. The front ends that served the CAPTCHAs were hosted on four servers: two on the East Coast and two on the West Coast. Eventually we added three servers in Europe for latency reasons— because of a big client that wanted low latency for their European users.

So we went from having a handful of servers that we had to manage ourselves to having as many resources as we wanted. In the first year or two at Google, we easily scaled up our traffic by six to eight times what it had been before.

When we got acquired, we were serving maybe four or five thousand CAPTCHAS per second. Which is not bad. Facebook used reCAPTCHA. So did Ticketmaster, Twitter, and a bunch of sites that were a big deal ten years ago and that nobody remembers anymore.

But within a year at Google, we were easily double or triple that. Not due to us doing any special marketing or anything. It was just organic growth from the sites that were already using us, plus others saying, "Okay, they're part of Google now, so they're not going to just disappear."

Which I guess is different than what people say when startups get acquired by Google these days!

These days, when they buy a startup, they usually just burn it down so it doesn't become a competitor.
Yeah.

You mentioned that Google Books had already scanned millions of books. Where did those books come from originally?
By the time we arrived, Google Books had been going on for years. It was first announced back in 2004. All of the book scanning was done in collaboration with libraries. Harvard and the University of Michigan were the two largest ones in the U.S.

The way it worked was that books that weren't checked out would get trucked off from the library to a Google scan center. There, they had people turning the pages and taking photos with cameras from above to scan them, to ensure it was a nondestructive scanning process.

I did get to see a scan center at one point. It's one of the first situations that I became aware of where Google was using TVCs.* Google wasn't directly employing the people scanning the books—there was some third party that was responsible for the scan center operations at any given place.

---

* TVCs are temps, vendors, and contractors. This is Google's term for its contingent workforce.

Libraries liked the project, because their whole point was the preservation of written material. So preserving that material digitally for future generations seemed good. And the libraries got the scans of the books to do whatever they wanted to with them.

What was the original impetus for the project?
My best guess is that Larry Page just thought it would be cool. He probably decided it was worth doing because compared to the scale of Google, the amount of resources required was not huge. And it made sense given Google's culture and mission back in 2004. Google was a search engine. The reasoning that I always heard was, "So you can search the web, but there's a whole bunch of human knowledge that's stuck in dead-tree form. Why can't you search all of that as well?"

The Culture Is Changing

I'm curious about your evolution in how you saw the company. When you first joined, you were excited. Suddenly you had a huge amount of computing power at your disposal, and you were part of this big, ambitious project to digitize the world's books. How did that feeling evolve over time?
Many different things changed at Google, both culturally and engineering-wise, over the nine years I was there.

The Google of nine years ago felt much closer to Larry

and Sergey's original vision. It was honest techno-utopianism. Google Books was a great example of that. "We're just going to try and scan all the world's books because we did some numbers on the back of an envelope and it seemed like we could." And they did actually scan 20 percent of all the books that had ever been published!*

When I started, Eric Schmidt was in charge. He seemed fine with having a loose, university-style atmosphere. Different teams worked on different things. Some of them succeeded and some of them didn't. But the company made a ridiculous amount of money from Search so it didn't really matter that much.

Then Larry Page became CEO in 2011, and things started to change.

How?

He introduced a lot more structure and hierarchy. Previously, there were relatively few divisions. Most projects were under Search—one might be web search, another might be book search. Larry reorganized the company into major product areas. Search was a division, but not the only one; there was also Android, Cloud, and so on. And he put a senior vice president in charge of each of them.

Right away, there was less of that university atmosphere where you could just walk up and talk to anybody

---

* By late 2015, Google had scanned more than twenty-five million books from more than a hundred countries, in four hundred different languages. According to Google, there are approximately 130 million published books in the world.

about their project and maybe help them out with it. Now the decisions were coming down from the senior vice president who was in charge of that product area. And those decisions were being driven by business objectives: overall, the company started caring more about the business and less about whimsical projects. Google started to become more like a typical big company.

You mentioned that you first encountered TVCs when working on Google Books. As the company began to change and become more corporate, did you notice more and more contractors around?

I can't think of a specific moment where there was a sudden influx. But percentage-wise, more and more of Google became temporary workers. It's now a majority— Google employs more TVCs than full-time employees.* It was probably 10 or 20 percent when I started.

At first, the introduction of TVCs seemed justified. Google is not in the business of hiring people to do everything. It doesn't have the time. So having some third party manage that seemed like it made sense. But over time, Google has gone from, "There's this special project that needs a few hundred people who have skill sets that no Googler currently has," to taking full-time positions and turning them into temporary or contract positions.

---

* According to *The New York Times*, Google employed 121,000 TVCs and 102,000 full-time employees by March 2019.

For example?

Recruiters. I had some awareness of this when I arrived, because it was in the middle of the Great Recession. Before, recruiters were full-time employees. But after the financial crisis, they scaled down hiring and basically fired a bunch of people because they had nothing to do. Then when they spun hiring back up again, résumé screeners and college recruiting coordinators were hired on a temporary basis. I remember older employees who had been there longer than me grumbling about it. They used to know the recruiting folks in this office or that office. Then they started turning over every year or two.

It makes everyone's life worse. That's the point. I worked on one project where we hired a third-party design firm to do the web design for a data visualization that we were gonna release publicly. And that was incredibly obnoxious from an engineering perspective because they can't see our code base. So I'm writing some stuff and they're writing some stuff and when we stick it together it's a giant mess because we're not all developing in the same place.

In addition to more hierarchy and more contractors, what were some of the other elements that started to change how you felt about the company?

The first thing that occurs to me is Google Plus.

Google Plus was meant to be a social networking competitor of Facebook. From the start, a decision was made that people were going to have to use their real names on

Google Plus. A bunch of Googlers then pointed out that this policy was problematic for a bunch of reasons. Trans people may be known by different names in different contexts. Sex workers might not feel safe using their real name. More generally, anybody who doesn't want to be automatically doxing* themselves for the opinions they post on the internet might not want to use their real name.

Why did management want real names?

Their main argument was that anonymous discourse on the internet is toxic. The idea was that if you made people sign up with their real name, there would be less bad online behavior, less trolling.

I very specifically remember an exec making an analogy to a restaurant. When you go to a nice restaurant, you have to wear a shirt and pants. If you want to eat at home, you can eat wearing whatever you want. But as members of polite society, we accept certain restrictions.

The analogy landed extremely poorly on a bunch of people internally. These execs have millions of dollars and are basically public figures. Of course they don't have a problem with using their real names, so they couldn't possibly imagine why anyone wouldn't want to. Also, from a logical standpoint, their argument didn't make a lot of sense. You can come up with an alias that looks like a real name and post the most toxic stuff in the world. It's

---

* Doxing is the practice of collecting and publishing an individual's personal information on the internet, typically with malicious intent.

not violating the names policy that's the problem—it's the behavior you're engaging in.

So what happened?

It took a while, but Googlers were able to push back and get the policy changed. It ended up in the state that I think should have been the state initially: you can type anything you want into the name field, so long as it's not offensive or you're not impersonating anyone. In fact, I remember one particular instance in which we disabled Neil Gaiman's account for impersonating Neil Gaiman! He escalated on Twitter, and Googlers went and fixed it.

It sounds like the real-names policy on Google Plus was an early example of a rift between rank-and-file Googlers and management.

Yes. Although in the subsequent years, many more rifts manifested and grew wider. Because back then, the feedback mechanism within Google was still working. There was still a measure of trust.

People on the Internet Are Jerks

When did that trust start to break down?

The Damore memo was definitely a turning point.

In July 2017, James Damore wrote and circulated his memo. He was fired the following month. Soon after, there were all these leaks of conversations within Google that got sent to his lawyers—screenshots of email threads or internal Google Plus threads. A lot of the posts had nothing to do with the memo. In many cases, they were written years before the memo. But Damore's legal counsel used them to make Google look like one big evil leftist conspiracy.

Then the leaks ended up on right-wing sites. A bunch of Googlers found themselves getting doxed and getting death threats. A lot of people were pretty scared. People's photos were getting posted on 4chan and Stormfront and 8chan and all these other terrible sites.* A bunch of well-known alt-right provocateurs, including Vox Day and Milo Yiannopoulos and various others on *Breitbart*, were involved.

What was the reaction to all of that within Google?
We were completely blindsided. There had never been any culture of leaking internal posts to score political points before. Or of people getting doxed and threatened. And the company didn't know how to deal with it.

Google has a physical security group that is very responsive. If there is an earthquake or a natural disaster or something, they call all the Googlers in the area to ensure they're safe and to provide help if needed. But for this kind of online attack, they didn't have a clue what to do.

Initially, there was no official support from Google for

---

* 4chan and 8chan are message boards popular with the alt-right, while Stormfront is a long-running neo-Nazi forum.

the Googlers who were affected. We got sent some use-less stock resources that told us not to use our real name and address online—ironic, given the Google Plus con-troversy. Nobody seemed to have any idea what the hell was going on.

Was there any kind of response from upper management?
Google's lawyers made the argument that the court should redact employees' names because they weren't rel-evant to the lawsuit. Eventually the judge agreed, and the docs that were leaked were retroactively redacted from the official court website.

But by then the screenshots were all over the most toxic parts of the right-wing internet. You can't remove stuff once it's gotten out there. Some Googlers put to-gether a letter to management asking for more resources for keeping the workplace safe. Basic things, like having codes of conduct on internal mailing lists that were un-moderated. But the letter was largely ignored.

Were many people you worked with sympathetic to Damore?
I don't know the numbers. Nobody I worked closely with. On some mailing lists, there were certainly people who took his firing as proof that Google was biased against conservative employees. Of course, the downside of Goo-gle's mailing list culture is that it's easy for twenty or thirty people to troll every thread.

How would you characterize the politics of people within Google, and within the tech industry more broadly?

Tech has an eclectic mix of political beliefs.

I would say that most rank-and-file people in tech tend to be on the liberal or socialist side of the spectrum. They believe in democratic institutions and government and things like that. But then you also have very libertarian people. For them, governments are bad at understanding technology. Therefore any regulation will be unhelpful or misguided or even straight-up malicious. Governments shouldn't try to regulate technology, so it's useless—or worse—for them to try.

Then you have the actual executives of these companies, who are often socially liberal but very fiscally conservative. They're multimillionaires or billionaires, so they would rather not pay taxes. They do everything that they can to reduce the taxes that the corporation pays and the taxes that they personally pay, because it's a huge chunk of their net worth.

The politics of tech mostly falls into this tripartite division.

It's hard to separate the Damore controversy from the political context of the 2016 election and its aftermath, which really energized the alt-right and the other right-wing elements that you described. But in that same period, you also start to see a more critical mood about tech and a sharper tone toward Silicon Valley from

**mainstream journalists and politicians—a cultural
shift that is sometimes called the "techlash" today.
How did that shift manifest within Google?**

As long as I can remember, there was always a basic recognition within Google that big tech companies have real
power—that their decisions can affect the geopolitics of
the whole world. In 2010, very early in my tenure at Google,
the company pulled out of China because the Chinese Com-
munist Party was hacking into Gmail accounts belonging
to dissidents and reporters.* Up to that point, Google had
been offering censored search results on Google.cn. In response to the hacking, the company said they would start
providing uncensored search results or nothing at all—
which quickly became nothing at all.

So it was always clear that what we did mattered. And
that recognition was what motivated the rank-and-file
campaign around the Google Plus real-names policy: people saw that there were downsides to the policy that would
negatively affect certain groups.

But I would say that 2016 and the aftermath brought
these issues into much sharper focus. Algorithmic news
feeds, fake news, content that's misleading or scammy or
worse—Cambridge Analytica is one famous example.†

---

* While Google offered a Chinese-language version of its search engine as early as 2000, it didn't officially launch Google.cn until January
2006. Google.cn provided censored search results, in compliance with
Chinese government regulations, until it closed in 2010.
† Cambridge Analytica was a British consulting firm that worked
on political campaigns around the world, including Donald Trump's

Overall, there was more and more of an understanding within Google and within the tech industry more generally of the consequences of what our companies were building. And it felt like a real departure from the old techno-utopian idea that if you just provide access to information, everything will turn out great. People on the internet are jerks. You have to design your systems with the assumption that hostile actors are going to try to use them to do bad things in various ways. And those actors aren't always just individual assholes. They're often part of large, well-coordinated groups. We're in the middle of a planetary information war.

Do the Right Thing

How did that greater understanding of the consequences of what the tech industry was building feed into the rank-and-file campaigns within Google against Project Maven and Dragonfly?*

This returns to our discussion earlier about the reorganization of the company that started after Larry Page be-

---

presidential bid in 2016. In March 2018, revelations about the extent of the firm's data-harvesting operations on Facebook caused a major scandal.

* Dragonfly was a search engine prototype being developed within Google to enable its reentry into the Chinese market. It returned censored search results and recorded users' searches. In August 2018, *The Intercept* published a leaked internal memo about Dragonfly, which is how many Googlers discovered the existence of the project. Following the disclosure, workers mounted a campaign to shut down Dragonfly.

came CEO in 2011, and which continued when Sundar Pichai took over in 2015.

The way the company was restructured into different divisions with distinct product areas changed the incentives when it came to pursuing controversial projects like reopening Search in China or working with the U.S. Department of Defense.

Take the Department of Defense. One of the divisions is Google Cloud. They want to be number one in cloud computing. They want to beat Amazon and Microsoft and the other competitors in the market. So for the senior vice president in charge of that division, it's a no-brainer to take military contracts. At the end of the day, what matters is increasing revenue for that division.

The early Google was different. Back then, it was clear that 90 percent of Google was Search, and everything else was free fun stuff that would eventually redirect people to Search. So you could make the argument that if Google engages in projects that compromise its credibility, people will trust Google less, and Search revenue will go down. Now that the company is split up into these separate fiefdoms, it's harder to make that case. Cloud doesn't really care if they take a controversial contract that undermines trust in Search.

By the same token, I'd imagine there's less room for projects like Google Books in the new structure.
Yeah. It's more hierarchical and has less of that academic feel. The number of engineers and product managers and

designers that you can have working on your project is driven by the business case for that project. It's far less of the freewheeling atmosphere of, "Sure, we can have ten or fifty people working on this experimental thing without knowing whether there's revenue there or not."

So there are fewer organic projects growing out of the curiosity of small teams. The direction is coming from the top and reflects specific business objectives, such as the need to break into this market or beat this competitor.

In the earlier situation with Google Plus, you said that the feedback mechanism was working. Employees raised their concerns and were able to make a change. By contrast, the rank-and-file campaigns around Dragonfly and Project Maven looked a lot different. They were bigger, more combative, and even spilled into the media. What changed?

In the Google Plus situation, there was an escalation path and a dialogue between rank-and-file workers and upper management. It was mediated by a senior engineer on the project who served as a kind of liaison. He would answer the questions about the real-names policy at TGIF, Google's weekly all-hands meeting, with a level of candor and humanness that the other execs did not really exude.

It was clear that he understood the reason people had problems. He was willing to compromise—even if there were challenges, even if it was going to take a while. He also had credibility on both sides: as one of the project's technical leaders, he was trusted by the rank-and-file engineers, but he was also trusted by upper management. Management was used to respecting his technical decisions, so they respected his arguments about other aspects of the project as well.

He left Google a couple of years ago. When he did, we lost a good liaison between the two sides. But as Google has gotten larger, I also think there's a growing feeling among the executives that this kind of back-and-forth isn't worth it. They feel impatient. They don't have time.

Presumably the reorganization you've been describing amplifies this tendency. In a more hierarchical structure, executives can rely more on directives than dialogue.

Sundar has said on more than one occasion that Google doesn't run the company by referendum. Which is not something that anybody has actually asked for! It's a very strange response to employee concerns.

The point is not necessarily to make every decision democratically but to at least help employees understand the reasons *why* a decision has been made. Then they're free to disagree, and can refuse to work on the project, or even leave the company. But these days, the answers from management just come across as business-speaky and vague. They try to placate people without actually showing that they've understood the substance of the concerns that have been raised. That makes it hard to feel heard, or even to know your own feelings about a specific project.

Do you think that your feelings about certain projects would have been different if the executives had done a better job of explaining the reasoning behind them?
Dragonfly is one where I could see an ethical gray area. We were building a search engine that gave the Chinese government the ability to censor certain topics and pages, and to surveil specific citizens and their searches.

On the other hand, people in China currently use Baidu, which is not very good.* It returns all kinds of wrong answers about medical information that they search for. We know that's a problem. We know they're not going to get effective treatment. Baidu is bad for their health. So you could argue that if Google provided better search results with better medical knowledge, the Chinese people using our search engine would be healthier and live longer lives.

I could see plausible arguments on either side. I could even line up on the side of Dragonfly being a net good if Google leadership had showed signs that they had understood and thought about these ethical issues ahead of time instead of after the fact—only after people raised concerns. After you've already built the prototype is not really the

---

* Baidu dominates the search engine market in China, and is the second-largest search engine in the world after Google.

time to start thinking about the ethical ramifications. And the arguments that were actually presented by the executives were very bad. Like, as a college freshman I would've been able to tell that they weren't valid arguments.

It seems like the gap between rank-and-file Googlers and upper management is growing pretty dramatically in this period.

A lot of what was missing was the mediation aspect. With Google Plus, we had somebody who could act as a go-between. We had an escalation path for concerns. You could send an email and get a response.

I have never once received a response to an email that I wrote to a Google executive who is on the board now. It just doesn't happen. They're busy people. Maybe they read it, maybe they don't. Either way, it's not a useful mechanism for feedback. And as the company and the number of controversies have grown so much larger, the all-hands meeting has become much less useful. You can't have a dialogue if all you get to do is ask one question every week or two.

It's also become harder to know who to even ask. When Dragonfly first became widely known internally, it wasn't clear who was running the project. This felt intentional: the execs went into panic mode when Dragonfly was discovered, so they stonewalled. It wasn't clear who you could ask questions of other than Sundar, and that remained the case for the first month or so that we knew about it. It is extremely weird not to have an escalation path that doesn't involve going up the org chart to your CEO.

But the worker-led campaigns did produce real changes. Google appears to have pulled back from Dragonfly, saying they have no plans to launch a search engine in China. In the summer of 2018, Google announced that it would not renew its contract with the Pentagon for Project Maven. And later that year, Google dropped out of the bidding war for Joint Enterprise Defense Infrastructure [JEDI], a major cloud computing contract with the Pentagon.
I have a friend whose opinion is that Google strongly believes in doing the right thing—so long as it doesn't cost Google money.

Honestly, I don't know what the right level of cynicism is. With the JEDI contract, Google probably wouldn't have won anyway because Amazon is so heavily favored.* So, when the employee advocacy started, the execs might have figured they could placate the workers by not competing for something that they weren't going to win anyway.

---

* On October 25, 2019, the Pentagon awarded the JEDI contract to Microsoft. Amazon lawyers filed a lawsuit to challenge the move, alleging that President Trump's personal hostility toward Amazon and its CEO, Jeff Bezos, led him to interfere in the procurement process. In February 2020, a federal judge ordered Microsoft to stop working on JEDI until Amazon's suit is resolved; the following month, the Pentagon asked the court to let it reconsider aspects of its contract, which was granted. As this book goes to press, the future of JEDI is unclear.

Do you think Google executives are still looking for ways to placate? It seems like the tone has grown more hostile than that.*

There's definitely been a major loss of trust on both sides. One way this manifests is through leaking: information that would have previously remained confidential keeps getting leaked to media outlets.

This creates a vicious cycle. Execs feel like they can't say anything useful because anything they say might end up on Twitter. And workers don't feel listened to because the execs aren't saying anything useful—which then makes them more likely to try methods of pressure that don't involve keeping the conversation inside the company.

If I were Google leadership I don't know how I would break this cycle. It's probably mathematically impossible at this point.

Presumably leaking can be impulsive: someone gets mad, and they talk to a reporter. But you're saying that it can also be strategic. What's the strategy?

Media pressure is currently among the most useful forms of pressure that workers can exert on Google. They try

---

* In April 2019, two of the organizers of the Google walkout, Claire Stapleton and Meredith Whittaker, went public with claims that they were facing retaliation from management for their role in the action; Stapleton left the company in June 2019, with Whittaker to follow shortly after in July. In November 2019, *The New York Times* reported that Google had hired a consulting firm that specializes in union busting. The same month, management fired four employees who were active in worker organizing.

to inflict a PR hit on the company for doing controversial things.

This can also affect hiring and retention. If Google is seen by engineers who have many job prospects as a place that's doing uncool or unethical work, people will simply take another job elsewhere. It'll be harder for Google to get talent and in some cases to retain the existing talent because people object to these projects.

A Deep Bench

Do you think that Google has been particularly fertile ground for white-collar worker organizing compared with other big tech companies? It seems like management's sensitivity to bad PR on the one hand and the relatively open internal culture on the other have played important enabling roles in these campaigns. I'm not sure the environment would be quite as favorable at a place like Amazon, for example.

Google certainly is its own separate world in terms of company culture. I get the feeling from folks at Amazon or Microsoft or other places that they have fewer company-wide forums in which rank-and-file employees can express their displeasure about something.

To be clear, these forums aren't just about social or political or product issues. There are many mailing lists that anybody can join. There are mailing lists for people who like skiing and people who like video games and people who like music. There are mailing lists for people who are trying to go walk their dogs together every Thursday or whatever.

So Google's culture does seem somewhat unique in that way. The mailing lists make it easy to quickly organize a couple hundred to a couple thousand people around an issue. You saw that with all of the worker campaigns, going back to Google Plus. The feeling that I get from workers at other companies is that this sort of culture doesn't exist elsewhere.

Ultimately, you decided to leave the company. Can you tell us why?

At some point, it felt like the controversies were stacking up faster than we could handle them. I could have made the decision to ignore them and just go heads-down on my engineering work. For a while, I tried.

Over the years, even as my feelings about the company grew more complicated, I had felt an ethical duty to stay and to continue doing what I could to push for changes in the direction of certain projects. I knew that I could apply more pressure from within the company than from outside. But eventually it felt like there was no way that I could usefully participate in that process. I lost faith that my opinions would be reflected in product decisions anymore. So I decided to leave.

Other people made different choices. Some people resigned much sooner. Some people are still around. One reason I felt all right about leaving, in fact, was because we've got a deep bench now. It's far from over. There are a lot of people inside who are going to keep pushing.

5

The Data Scientist

Ever since the region first emerged as an industrial zone after World War II, Silicon Valley has been reinventing itself. It was once known for microchips and mainframes. Then came personal computers and the web. These days, artificial intelligence looms large. Companies are investing heavily in AI and snapping up all the AI experts they can find. The next incarnation of Silicon Valley, it seems fair to say, will revolve around AI—if it doesn't already.

But what even is AI? This should be a simple question, but honest answers are surprisingly hard to find. Mystification and misinformation abound, amplified by a media that's typically far too deferential to industry hype. We're told that AI is about to revolutionize everything—among other things, by throwing millions of people out of work by automating away their jobs.

This didn't sound quite right to us, so we sat down with a veteran data scientist to learn more. The data scientist helped us sort the fact from the fiction, and obtain a clearer view of Silicon Valley's *next* next big thing. When you strip away all the nonsense, what's actually going on?

All right, let's get started with the basics. What is a data scientist? Do you self-identify as one?

I would say the people who are the most confident about self-identifying as data scientists are almost unilaterally frauds. They are not people you would voluntarily spend a lot of time with.

There are a lot of people in this category who have only been exposed to a little bit of real stuff—they're sort of peripheral. You actually see a lot of this with these strong AI companies: companies that claim to be able to build human intelligence using some inventive "Neural Pathway Connector Machine System," or something.* You can look at the profiles of every single one of these companies. There are always people who have strong technical credentials, and they are in a field that is just slightly adjacent to AI, like physics or electrical engineering.

And that's close, but the issue is that no person with a Ph.D. in AI starts one of these companies, because if you get a Ph.D. in AI, you've spent years building a bunch of really shitty models, or you see robots fall over again and again and again. You become so acutely aware of the limitations of what you're doing that the interest just gets beaten out of you. You would never go and say, "Oh, yeah, I know the secret to building human-level AI."

---

* Strong AI is the paradigm of trying to model and build human intelligence in a machine. Specific or applied AI, on the other hand, tries to build a method for getting really good at solving a more narrow set of problems.

In a way it's sort of like my dad, who has a Ph.D. in biology and is a researcher back east, and I told him a little bit about the Theranos story.* I told him their shtick: "Okay, you remove this small amount of blood, and run these tests . . ." He asked me what the credentials were of the person starting it, and I was like, "She dropped out of Stanford undergrad." And he was like, "Yeah, I was wondering, since the science is just not there." Only somebody who never actually killed hundreds of mice and looked at their blood—like my dad did—would ever be crazy enough to think that was a viable idea.

So I think a lot of the strong AI stuff is like that. A lot of data science is like that, too. Another way of looking at data science is that it's a bunch of people who got Ph.D.s in the wrong thing, and realized they wanted to have a job. Another way of looking at it—I think the most positive way, which is maybe a bit contrarian—is that it's really, really good marketing.

As someone who tries not to sell fraudulent solutions to people, it actually has made my life significantly better because you can say "big data machine learning," and people will be like, "Oh, I've heard of that, I want that." It makes it way easier to sell them something than having to explain this complex series of mathematical operations. The hype around it—and *that* there's so much hype—has

---

* Theranos was a health technology company that promised a new way to collect and test blood samples. After a series of investigations exposed its technology as fraudulent, the company imploded.

made the actual sales process so much easier. The fact that there is a thing with a label is really good for me professionally.

But that doesn't mean there's not a lot of ridiculous hype around the discipline.

I'm curious about the origins of the term "data science"—do you think that it came internally from people marketing themselves, or that it was a random job title used to describe someone, or what?
As far as I know, the term "data science" was invented by Jeff Hammerbacher at Facebook.

The Cloudera guy?*
Yeah, the Cloudera guy. As I understand it, "data science" originally came from the gathering of data on his team at Facebook.

If there was no hype and no money to make, essentially, what I would say data science is, is the fact that the data sets have gotten large enough where you can start to consider variable interactions in a way that's becoming increasingly predictive. And there are a number of problems where the actual individual variables themselves don't have a lot of meaning, or they are kind of ambiguous, or they are only very weak signals. There's information in the

---

* Cloudera is an enterprise big data company that supports and sells a platform for using Apache Hadoop, an open-source framework for distributed data storage and processing.

correlation structure of the variables that can be revealed, but only through really huge amounts of data.

So essentially, there are n variables, right? So there's n-squared potential correlations, and n-cubed potential cubic interactions or whatever. Right? There's a ton of interactions. The only way you can solve that is by having massive amounts of data.

So the data scientist role emphasizes the data part first. It's like, we have so much data, and so this new role arises using previous disciplines or skills applied to a new context?

You can start to see new things emerge that would not emerge from more standard ways of looking at problems. That's probably the most charitable way of putting it without any hype. But I should also say that the hype is just ferocious.

And even up until recently, there's just massive bugs in the machine-learning libraries that come bundled with Spark.* It's so bizarre, because you go to Caltrain [Bay Area commuter rail line], and there's a giant banner showing a cool-looking data scientist peering at computers in some cool ways, advertising Spark, which is a platform that in my day job I know is just barely usable at best, or at worst, actively misleading.

---

* Spark is a distributed platform for data applications whose main benefit is the ability to process data in memory, which is much faster than applications that must more frequently read data from disk.

I don't know. I'm not sure that you can tell a clean story that's completely apart from the hype.

For people who are less familiar with these terms, how would you define "data science," "machine learning," and "AI"? Because as you mentioned, these are terms that float around a lot in the media and that people absorb, but it's unclear how they fit together.

It's a really good question. I'm not even sure if those terms that you referenced are on solid ground themselves.

I'm friends with a venture capitalist who became famous for coining the phrase "machine intelligence," which is pretty much just the first word of "machine learning" with the second word of "artificial intelligence," and as far as I can tell is essentially impossible to distinguish from either of those applications.

I would say, again, "data science" is really shifty. If you wanted a pure definition, I would say data science is much closer to statistics. "Machine learning" is much more predictive optimization, and "AI" is increasingly hijacked by a bunch of yahoos and Elon Musk types who think robots are going to kill us. I think "AI" has gotten too hot as a term. It has a constant history since the dawn of computing of overpromising and substantially underdelivering.

So do you think when most people think of AI, they think of strong AI?

They think of the film *Artificial Intelligence*, that level of AI, yeah. And as a result, I think people who are familiar with bad robots falling over shy away from using that term, just because they're like, "We are nowhere near that." Whereas a lot of people who are less familiar with shitty robots falling over will say, "Oh, yeah, that's exactly what we're doing."

The narrative around automation is so present right now in the media, as you know. I feel like all I read about AI is how self-driving trucks are going to put all these truckers out of business. I know there's that Oxford study that came out in 2013 that said some insane percentage of our jobs are vulnerable to automation.* How should we view that? Is that just the outgrowth of a really successful marketing campaign? Does it have any basis in science, or is it just hype?

Can I say the truth is halfway there? I mean, again, I want to emphasize that historically, from the very first moment somebody thought of computers, there has been a notion of, "Oh, can the computer talk to me, can it learn to love?" And somebody, some yahoo, will be like, "Oh, absolutely!" And then a bunch of people will put money into it, and then they'll be disappointed.

And that's happened so many times. In the late 1980s,

---

* Carl Benedikt Frey and Michael A. Osborne, "The Future of Employment" (September 17, 2013), https://www.oxfordmartin.ox.ac.uk /downloads/academic/future-of-employment.pdf. Frey and Osborne estimate that 47 percent of total U.S. employment is at risk of computerization. Their claims are controversial, however, and have been challenged from a number of directions.

there was a huge Department of Defense research effort toward building a Siri-like interface for fighter pilots. And of course this was thirty years ago and they just massively failed. They failed so hard that DARPA was like, "We're not going to fund any more AI projects."* That's how bad they fucked up. I think they actually killed Lisp as a programming language—it died because of that. There are very few projects that have failed so completely that they actually killed the programming language associated with them.

The other one that did that was the—what was it, the Club of Rome or something?† Where they had those growth projections in the 1970s about how we were all going to die by now. And it killed the modeling language they used for the simulation. Nobody can use that anymore because the earth has been salted with how shitty their predictions were.

It's like the name Benedict.

Yes, exactly, or the name Adolf. Like, you just don't go there.

---

* Defense Advanced Research Projects Agency, the advanced R&D wing of the Department of Defense. Over the decades, the agency has funded the development of many breakthrough technologies, including the internet.

† *The Limits to Growth* is a 1972 report commissioned by the Club of Rome, a European NGO, that predicted rapid declines in global population and industrial capacity beginning in the early twenty-first century.

So, I mean, that needs to be kept in mind. Anytime anybody promises you an outlandish vision about what AI is, you just absolutely have to take it with a grain of salt, because this time is not different.

Is there a point at which a piece of software or a robot officially becomes "intelligent"? Does it have to pass a certain threshold to qualify as intelligent? Or are we just making a judgment call about when it's intelligent?

I think it's irrelevant in our lifetimes and in our grand-children's lifetimes. It's a very good philosophical question, but I don't think it really matters. I think that we are going to be stuck with specific AI for a very, very long time.

And what is specific AI?

Optimization around a specific problem, as opposed to optimization on every problem.

So, like, driving a car would be a specific problem?

Yeah. Whereas if we invented a brain that we can teach to do anything we want, and we have chosen to have it focus on the specific vertical of driving a car, but it can be applied to anything, that would be general AI. But I think that would be literally making a mind, and that's almost irresponsible to speculate about. It's just not go-ing to happen in any of our lifetimes, or probably within the next hundred years. So I think I would describe it as philosophy. I don't know, I don't have an educated opinion about that.

Money Machines

One hears a lot about algorithmic finance, and things like robo-advisers.* And I'm wondering, does that fall into the same category of stuff that seems pretty over-hyped?

I would say that robo-advisers are not doing anything special. It's AI only in the loosest sense of the word. They're not really doing anything advanced—they're applying a formula. And it's a reasonable formula, it's not a magic formula. They're not quantitatively assessing markets and trying to make predictions. They're applying a formula about whatever stock and bond allocations to make—it's not a bad service, but it's super hyped. That's indicative of a bubble in AI that you have something like that where you're like, "It's AI!" and people are like, "Okay, cool!"

There's a function that's being optimized—which is, at some level, what a neural net is doing.† But it's not really AI.

I think one of the big tensions in data science that is

---

* Robo-advisers are systems that provide automated portfolio management advice.

† Artificial neural networks are the technology that forms the basis of the recent AI boom.

was just sitting there watching this game, like, I cannot believe it—it's either they don't know, which is terrifying, or they know and they don't give a shit, which is also terrifying.

I don't know how that court case is going to work out, but I can tell you in the next ten years, there's going to be a court case about it. And I would not be surprised if SoFi lost for discrimination. And in general, I think it's going to be an increasingly important question about the way that we handle protected classes generally, and maybe race specifically, in data science models of this type.* Because otherwise it's like, okay, you can't directly model if a person is black. Can you use their zip code? Can you use the racial demographics for the zip code? Can you use things that correlate with the racial demographics of their zip code? And at what level do you draw the line?

And we know what we're doing for mortgage lending— and the answer there is, frankly, a little bit offensive—which is that we don't give a shit where your house is. We just lend. That's what Rocket Mortgages does.† It's a fucking app, and you're like, "How can I get a million-dollar loan with an app?" And the answer is that they legally can't tell where your house is. And the algorithm that you use to do mortgages has to be vetted by a federal agency.

---

* A protected class is defined by U.S. federal antidiscrimination law as a group of people with a common characteristic who are legally protected from discrimination on the basis of that characteristic. The characteristics include race, religion, and gender.

† A service of Quicken Loans that offers an online mortgage service.

That's an extreme, but that might be the extreme we go down, where every single time anybody gets assessed for anything, the actual algorithm and the inputs are assessed by a federal regulator. So maybe that's going to be what happens. I actually view it a lot like the debates around divestment. You can say, "Okay, we don't want to invest in any oil companies," but then do you want to invest in things that are positively correlated with oil companies, like oil field services companies? What about things that in general have some degree of correlation? How much is enough?

I think it's the same thing where it's like, okay, you can't look at race, but can you look at correlates of race? Can you look at correlates of correlates of race? How far do you go down before you say, "Okay, that's okay to look at"?

I'm reminded a bit of Cathy O'Neil's book *Weapons of Math Destruction: How Big Data Increases Inequality and Threatens Democracy* [2016]. One of her arguments, which it seems like you're echoing, is that the popular perception is that algorithms provide a more objective, more complete view of reality, but that they often just reinforce existing inequities.

That's right. And the part that I find offensive as a mathematician is the idea that somehow the machines are doing something wrong. We as a society have not chosen to optimize for the thing that we're telling the machine to optimize for. That's what it means for the machine to be doing illegal things. The machine isn't doing anything wrong, and the algorithms are not doing anything wrong. It's just that they're literally amoral, and if we told them the things that are okay to optimize against, they would optimize against those instead. It's a frightening, almost *Black Mirror*–esque view of reality that comes from the machines, because a lot of them are completely stripped of—not to sound too Trumpian—liberal pieties. It's completely stripped.

They're not "politically correct."
They are massively not politically correct, and it's disturbing. You can load in tons and tons of demographic data, and it's disturbing when you see percent black in a zip code and percent Hispanic in a zip code be more important than borrower debt-to-income ratio when you run a credit model. When you see something like that, you're like, Ooh, that's not good. Because the frightening thing is that even if you remove those specific variables, if the signal is there, you're going to find correlates with it all the time, and you either need to have a regulator that says, "You can use these variables, you can't use these variables," or, I don't know, we need to change the law.

As a data scientist I would prefer if that did not come out in the data. I think it's a question of how we deal with it. But I feel sensitive toward the machines, because we're telling them to optimize, and that's what they're coming up with.

They're describing our society.

Yeah. That's right, that's right. That's exactly what they're doing. I think it's scary. I can tell you that a lot of the opportunity those fintech companies are finding is derived from that kind of discrimination, because if you are a large enough lender, you are going to be very highly vetted, and if you're a very small lender you're not.*

Take SoFi, for example. They refinance the loans of people who went to good colleges. They probably did not set up their business to be super racist, but I guarantee you they are super racist in the way they're making loans, in the way they're making lending decisions.

Is that okay? Should a company like that exist?

I don't know. I can see it both ways. You could say, "They're a company, they're providing a service for people, people want it, that's good." But at the same time, we have such a shitty legacy of racist lending in this country. It's very hard not to view this as yet another racist lending policy, but now it's got an app.

When we talk about fintech in general, does that refer to something broader than advising investors when to buy and sell stocks, and this new sort of loaning behavior? Or is that the main substance of it?

Fintech may most accurately be described as regulatory arbitrage: startups are picking up pieces that a big bank

---

* Fintech is short for "financial technology," and it refers to a group of companies that are trying to use technology to transform financial services.

can't do, won't do, or that are just too small for it to pick up. And I think fintech is going to suffer over the next five years. If there's a single sector that people are going to be less enamored with in five years than they are now, fintech is definitely the one.

The other side of it is that they're exploiting a hack in the way venture capitalists think. Venture capital as an industry is actually incredibly small relative to the financial system. So if you were starting, I don't know, a company that used big data to make intelligent decisions on home loans—which is probably illegal, but whatever, you're small enough that it's no big deal—and you say, "Hey, we're doing ten million dollars a year in business," a venture capitalist will look at you like, "Holy shit, I've never seen a company get up to ten million dollars in business that fast." The venture capitalist has no idea that the mortgage market is worth trillions of dollars and the startup essentially has none of it. The founder gives a market projection like, "Oh, this is a trillion-dollar industry," and the venture capitalist is like, "Oh, that market is enormous. I've never seen numbers like that before."

It's much more of a clever hack than an actual, sustainable, lasting, value-creating enterprise. One of the biggest flagship fintech companies, LendingClub, is in a ton of trouble.* SoFi is probably illegal. And those are the flag bearers for the sector.

---

* LendingClub is a peer-to-peer lending company. In 2014, it went public in the year's largest U.S. tech company IPO; in 2016, a series of

The other thing that happened was the San Bernardino shootings—apparently the guns that were used were financed by a loan from Prosper, which is another peer-to-peer lender.* And you just think about where this is going to go. Are we eventually going to get to the point where we have the credit models to assess and not give that guy a loan because of the risk that he could be a Muslim terrorist? Is that the society that we will be living in?

Maybe. But we're going to get there with the data.

The Future

If you had to give a nontechnical layperson one piece of advice for thinking about these questions, what would it be? Is it to be more skeptical? Is it to be less credulous when confronted with hype? Because it seems like there's a fairly small number of people who understand these technologies well, and yet they appear to have the potential to make a pretty big impact on a lot of people's lives.

I think the most realistic way of looking at it is that it's not all hype. The technical advances are real—and even if they're not real today, the relentless drumbeat of

---

scandals drove its share price down nearly 85 percent, where it has more or less remained.

* On December 2, 2015, two attackers killed fourteen people and injured twenty-two others in a mass shooting at the Inland Regional Center in San Bernardino, California.

progress on hardware and algorithms will make them real eventually. It will take longer than you think— potentially a lot longer than you think—but it will happen. So everything you're hearing is an early warning sign of what the future is going to look like. Maybe not even in our lifetimes, but yeah, it'll get there. And the questions that we're going over, they're going to be real. It's just not there yet.

So yeah, I would recommend some skepticism, but not complete skepticism. Because the advances underlying this are real. And the rate of progress has kept up, and I don't see a reason why it's going to stop.

It's funny, because I think the biggest concern that I have for the future is that a bunch of people like me are going to make a bunch of money. And a bunch of people are going to lose their jobs. And a bunch of people are going to get new jobs that are crazy and cool. But I don't know on net how great it's going to be for society moving forward, though I want to be optimistic about it.

I often have this kind of discussion with people who are algorithmically minded, and they view capitalism as an optimizing function. And all questions about technological change go through this filter of, well, we're glad we have cars instead of horses and buggies. And everything else will sort itself out. But everything else doesn't just "sort itself out."

I mean, I try to not fall into the Y Combinator/Stanford guy thing, but I actually do think that universal basic income is going to be the endgame.* I think that is what society will look like long-term, because I think universal basic income is the welfare that everyone can get behind.

But it's such a weighty question, and technology's impact on the economy changes so quickly that I don't know if any of us have ever really had the chance to take a breath. You look at some of the strikes a hundred years ago, like at the Homestead plant, where the workers held out and had fucking gunboats come down the river with Pinkertons and shoot the shit out of people.† There's a Costco there now, and a bunch of smokestacks where the plant used to be. And it's like, was that whole thing just this ridiculous farce? I don't even know.

I feel like it's always a question of, what are you optimizing for?
I think the strangest thing about being out here in the Bay Area is that the worldview has just completely saturated everything to the point that people think that everything is a technical problem that should be solved technologically. It's a very privileged view of very smart people. It's troubling.

On the one hand, there's no better shepherd for the economy than an engineer; on the other hand, there's

---

* Y Combinator is an early-stage startup investor and accelerator.
† The Homestead steel strike was an 1892 labor dispute at Andrew Carnegie's Homestead steel mill, in Pennsylvania, involving violent clashes between union members and private security forces.

no worse shepherd for the economy than an engineer. Because that kind of machine thinking is very good at producing some things, and very, very bad at producing other things.

On the one hand, I don't view any of the Silicon Valley startup economies as producing any kind of sustainable growth or ways of employing all these people. On the other hand, I do think that the basic income idea eventually will be the future. One of the most interesting things is the amount of leverage that individual people in Silicon Valley are getting—you look at the WhatsApp acquisition or whatever, with so few people being worth so much money.

That may have been a little bit irrational, but longer term, it's hard to argue against. And I don't see another endgame other than pretty high taxes plus basic income as the way of making that okay, because I don't think that's going to go away. I'm not even totally sure that we should discourage it from happening.

This may be a tangent, but I think the technical mindset is very compatible with the technocratic mindset. In both cases, it's an evasion of politics, because just as the person who designs the racist algorithm presumably does not think of what they're doing as political, neither does the technocrat who crafts the free trade agreement because all the mainstream economists in the room told him it would be good for the economy, full stop.

I think both approaches are connected to this overwhelming need to see political problems as technical ones, whether from an engineering perspective or from a technocratic governance perspective. To me those feel totally compatible. What you're describing—the Silicon Valley view of the world—feels to me like a very technocratic view of the world, where if you can just solve certain problems, then it will benefit everyone.

In defense of it, it's also a hopeful view of the world, because you're at least trying to describe problems that you can solve. It's a very optimistic way of looking at things, and I'm hesitant to abandon that, because I think ultimately . . . it's hard, grappling with this idea of the enormous amount of individual leverage and the crazy rate of change.

On the other hand, it's hard not to be a kind of technical utopian. It's hard to bet against the innovation that this country has produced, and maybe that's a function of survivorship bias or looking back and saying we just happened to get lucky. But you know, airplanes, the elevator—we just invented that stuff, and that's kind of cool. And so it seems sort of melancholy—or maybe this is my own limitation as a technical thinker to see it as melancholy—to be like, "Yeah, there's some stuff we can't solve."

I'm not sure I want to live in that world. I always want to live in a world where we're at least trying. But we'll see.

6

The Massage Therapist

Janitors are on their feet all day. Engineers are at their computers all day. What does Silicon Valley do to the body? Nobody knows better than a massage therapist.

We spoke to someone who was paid to pummel and pry open the knotted muscles of tech's more privileged workers. Massage gave her an unusual window into the dynamics of the company where she worked, and those of the industry as a whole. She saw some people at their most vulnerable, others at their most insufferable. We talked about what tension feels like, and the various tensions of her own job. We talked about tech's unspoken hierarchies, and whether stress makes you a better worker.

How did you come to be a massage therapist in tech?
I trained in massage in my mid-forties. Soon after I graduated, I was recruited over LinkedIn by a wellness startup that had a contract to provide services to a large tech company. That company was our only client.

The model was data-driven wellness. Our startup was trying to provide meaningful metrics to the company to demonstrate that we were saving them money by preventing illness through offering massage, chiropractic, acupuncture, training, exercise, yoga—that sort of thing.

Employees could come to us and pay only a dollar to get a service.

How did you feel about working in tech?
My husband is a San Francisco native. Nobody in our family is in the tech industry. But we lived in Noe Valley. So I saw the Google bus phenomenon when it was just starting to happen. And I had read about Twitter getting a tax break from our city while I was pressured to raise inordinate amounts of money for my children's public school education.* So let's just say I had mixed feelings.

But when I was hired, I decided to set all that aside and try to take people as they were. When you're massaging somebody, you really don't care if they're rich or poor or anything like that. You just deal with the body in front of you.

Tell us about the bodies.
People worked long hours. They had postural problems, the sort you get from sitting at a desk all day. Many of them did not exercise or strengthen their body, so the wear and tear of being on a computer for ten to twelve

---

* In June 2011, the San Francisco Board of Supervisors approved a measure that removed the 1.5 percent payroll tax for all new jobs for six years if these jobs were created by companies that opened offices in the economically struggling Mid-Market area. The measure was popularly known as the "Twitter tax break," because it was designed to keep Twitter in the city after the company announced it was planning to relocate.

hours straight was even worse because they had muscle weakness. We also had people who would go home and game all night long and get three hours of sleep and come back to work and then wonder why they hurt all the time.

Mostly, though, people were just stressed out. So they had the muscle tension that comes with that.

What kind of tension is that?

Somebody might come in and say, "Oh, my shoulders feel a bit tight." And then as you start to work on their shoulders, it feels completely solid. Like their back is a single slab of marble. You cannot differentiate the different muscles from each other or even from the bones of the spine. Everything is tense in equal measure and everything feels the same.

Of course, it's incredibly tiring to apply pressure to a body like that. It's not so different from trying to soften up old meat. So you end up worrying about your hands. I have arthritis developing in a couple of my joints.

Tell us about the people who came in for massages. What were your interactions like?

Only direct employees of the company could use the service. I voiced a desire many times to work on the kitchen staff, who were contract workers like us. There was a young woman in the cafeteria who had lymphedema. It was congenital; she'd had it since she was a child. Her legs were huge. And I wanted to work on her because she had to stand or lean on a stool all day. Having a little bit of massage would have helped her tremendously. But she wasn't allowed.

So were most of the people you saw software engineers?
It was a mix. There were some difficult young men who came in and wanted to express their dominance. They were almost exclusively engineers. They would ask me a lot of questions about how I was trained and what I knew about the body. Quizzing me on my job while receiving a massage.

How would you respond?
I usually tried to rebalance things by answering their questions about my background and my training matter-of-factly, and then just stop talking. So they would realize that quizzing me was not the point of the massage. Sometimes I would just lean on the sore parts of their body. That's one fail-safe trick to get someone out of their head and back into the present.

One guy in particular stood out to me because he always insisted on taking off his shirt to get a massage. He was very hairy, and he seemed unaware that back hair is difficult to massage. He had just gone to his first Burning Man right around the time he joined the company, and he had just discovered CrossFit. He liked to talk about both. I remember him to this day. You never forget a hairy back.

What about the women?
There were a lot of female administrative staff. They tended to be physically fit, trim, attractive younger women.

Many of them seemed stressed and sad. It sent my antennae up. I felt protective. The vibe was that they always had to have a smile on their face. They had to joke along with the guys. They had to be smart and funny. They had to be entertaining. I worried about them.

All of the executives at the company had their own administrative assistants. I remember one woman in particular. She was gorgeous. She was in her twenties, twenty-eight at the most. She wasn't the assistant to the CEO, but to someone right below him. One day, she came in incredibly stressed. She had scheduled a thirty-minute massage for herself. She came in holding her phone, which was how her executive communicated with her. And when she lay down on the table, she wouldn't let go of it.

I don't just mean the phone was on the massage table with her. Plenty of other people did that, which was fine with me. I mean she was literally holding it during her session.

I tried to take it out of her hand and we nearly had a fight. When I reached for it, she yanked it back. I wanted to be maternal and caring, but also assertive. Like, you're not gonna get anything out of the massage if you're on the phone. There was a back-and-forth there for a second, a real tug-of-war. Finally, I thought: The horse is out of the barn. I guess she needs this phone. So I let go.

Feeling her body, I could tell that she was near some kind of break. Just physically and emotionally drained.

A few minutes later, something happened on her phone and she got up and ran out.

Invisible Lines

What did people talk about during their massages?
Would people tell you about their work? Did they see
you as someone they could confide in?

People almost never talked about work. I think they had all
been told to be careful with the massage therapists for fear
of spilling trade secrets. We were also all made to sign
an NDA before working there. One of the conditions was
that we couldn't even reveal the name of the company. I
mean, good Lord. My husband is a police detective. He
has a top-secret clearance from the federal government,
and he has more freedom to talk about where he worked
and what he did than I did at that company at the very same
time. He works on some sensitive stuff, like literal life-and-
death stuff. The whole thing was kind of ridiculous.

One time, there was a woman who came to see me for
a massage who was extremely upset. I think she worked in
HR. She just lay on the table and cried and cried. But she
wouldn't talk about whatever it was. The general rule in
massage is that when somebody is crying and they don't
want to talk about it, you just let them. So I didn't press it.

Then there was the time that I saw one of my regulars
in our area. So I came over with my breakfast tray and said
hello. He was on his laptop working, and his screen was
facing where I was standing. When he saw me, he quickly
turned his laptop away and slammed the screen down.
And I thought, Honey, nothing on that screen would mean
a thing to me. I mean, I wouldn't be able to understand
what I was looking at, let alone interpret any of the code.

**What was "your area"? Was the place where the
massage therapists worked cordoned off from the rest
of the company?**

We were technically allowed to go anywhere. I had the
badge to access all the different floors. But in practice,
there was an unspoken, self-policed hierarchy of who was
allowed to go where.

How did you experience that hierarchy?

There was a really incredible coffee bar on one of the
floors. The executive chef at the company was the person
who brought in our wellness startup. I think he had a
personal connection to one of the founders. For him, his
power base in the company lay in the food. So he told us
to go to the coffee bar anytime we wanted.

I went there a couple of times, but I never felt comfortable. No matter how many times they told us we could
and should go anywhere, I felt like if I ever ventured beyond our little corner of the company, people would just
start looking at me like, Who are you and why are you
here? You obviously don't fit. I remember feeling like there
were eyes in my back, eyes boring a hole in my back. If I
went too deep into a space, if I went over some invisible
line, I was like, I'd better turn around and go.

**Did you and your fellow massage therapists eat at the
company cafeteria?**

Yup. One of the perks of the job was that we got two free
meals there per day.

The galley where you would pick up your food was in

the center of the cafeteria. In a U shape around that galley was the seating area. All of the contract workers tended to gather at one of the top ends of the U. Not an ideal place to sit, but that's where we all felt safe. We could just kind of relax a little bit—the massage therapists, the kitchen staffers, the people who worked at the coffee bar and the juice bar. Not the janitorial staff, though, because they never got to sit down.

Did you ever sit with the full-time employees?
The massage therapists were sort of this in-between group in the office because we interfaced with a lot of engineers. They were mostly friendly to us. They treated us better than the kitchen staff, who definitely bore the brunt of the snobbish behavior. But they didn't want us to sit with them. It felt like high school.

Sometimes an engineer would drift too far into our part of the cafeteria and suddenly realize where he was and immediately pick up his tray and run back toward the other engineers.

The most uncomfortable manifestation of these unwritten rules was what happened with my daughter.

What happened?
One day, for some reason, I can't remember why, my daughter was at work with me. She was a fifth grader at the time and she had some interest in tech and computers and had learned to code over the summer. So I wanted to introduce her to a lovely young engineer, a woman, who

I had gotten to know. That woman was brilliant. She had been homeschooled, but I think she was a better coder than all the guys who had gone to the fancy Ivy League schools.

My daughter and I entered the engineering area. It was a big, open floor. There were maybe a hundred engineers at work. And I just remember feeling like I was walking through a fog of "No, get away." I can't totally explain it. There's nothing specific I can point to. I just felt unwelcome. I felt people's eyes on me. People looking at me like, Who is she and why is she here? And I had a child with me, which I'm sure was unusual.

Anyway, we made it to the desk of this young woman and her male coworker. They were hard at work at their standing desks. They were both very nice, although he seemed a bit uncomfortable. It was awkward. It felt like I had done something wrong. It made me realize that people can be nice, but that doesn't mean they necessarily want you in their space.

Do you think your daughter noticed?
No. But I felt so mortified for her. I felt ashamed. I'd clearly made some sort of mistake, some kind of social faux pas.

Later, I got angry. I didn't want my daughter to be exposed to any of that. That's fine for me, not for my kids. I didn't want my child to be touched by this hierarchical crap.

Does she still want to work in tech?
She does not.

Closing Time

Tell us about how you came to stop working in tech.

At some point, I began to realize that the company wasn't doing so well. I started to pick up on it with one of my favorites. He always treated me like a regular person. Not putting me on a pedestal, not treating me like a servant—he just took me as I was. And that was actually sort of an exception.

He was a little older than the average engineer, mid to late thirties. Just the sweetest teddy bear of a guy. The company had purchased a food delivery app, and it required a lot of integration, or something. They assigned him to the project, and it was a bumpy ride. Things didn't seem to be pulling together. He was working insane hours. His body was a wreck. The stress was killing him. His back felt like Sheetrock.

Did he ever talk about what exactly was going wrong?

As I said before, I'm sure they were told not to discuss business, because almost nobody did. And I didn't want to know. I would never want to carry trade secrets around in my head. I had too much to do. But I knew that whatever was happening, it wasn't good.

Things were failing left and right. This was around the time that people started to talk about the company going public. Then it just stopped. The fizzling of the IPO created a sense of upheaval. People started worrying about the potential for layoffs. The stress level definitely picked up. It drove a lot of traffic to our wellness center.

That's also when our wellness startup started to get mixed signals about its relationship with the tech company.

How did that go down?
After the failed IPO, the tech company brought in someone new to run HR. And that person terminated the contract with the wellness startup.

Do you know why?
The startup's founders talked to me a lot. They said they routinely got feedback that we were so good at our jobs that the engineers were coming back to work *too* relaxed. So maybe that played a role in the demise of the program. Maybe stress and tension really do make you a better worker.

7

The Storyteller

Among Silicon Valley's chief exports are the stories it tells about itself. Every company needs a founding myth—extra points if it involves a garage. But as critical scrutiny of the industry has increased, storytelling has acquired a new urgency. More than ever, companies need to justify themselves and their actions to politicians and regulators and journalists and the general public, as well as to their own employees.

The people who perform this work fall into a range of roles: communications, marketing, and public policy, among others. But their function is broadly similar. They help the company speak, and ensure that it speaks in a single voice.

We talked to someone who, until recently, told these kinds of stories for a living. They helped us understand how Silicon Valley speaks, both to itself and to the world.

⁛

What was your most recent role in the tech industry?
My job was to tell the right story for bringing a product to market. Let's say there's a new product, or a new feature of an existing product, that the company wanted to launch. I helped craft a strategy for midwifing it into the world. My

goal was to come up with a way to talk about the product in such a way that it would not be misunderstood.

What does it mean for a product to be misunderstood?
My job was at a high-profile company that can be closely scrutinized by the public and by the press. Its products can easily be misunderstood by external parties: by users, policymakers, journalists. So it was important to tell the story in a way that accurately conveyed the benefits but also factored in the risks.

If there are aspects of a new user experience that could be perceived as self-serving for the company, or only appreciated by a subsection of its users, those kinds of misperceptions need to be anticipated and mitigated with thoughtful messaging.

Could you give an example?
Imagine a new feature that's designed to make messaging more private. If it's good for privacy, it might not be so good for safety. So certain privacy and human rights advocates might like it but parents and safety groups and law enforcement might not. You have to start with the stakeholders. Who is going to care about this? Who is going to be most affected? Whose stakes need to be understood and analyzed and managed?

When it comes to telling the story, it's almost like architecting a screenplay. You need to know who your protagonist is. This might be the person who is going to benefit from your feature—or the entire community at large. Or it might be the person who led the development of the feature within the company.

But you don't get the length of a screenplay, obviously. You have to be concise. You have a press release, or really just the headline of a press release, because that's what positions the whole launch. Or you have the text that pops up in the app when someone tries to use the feature. That language is heavily labored over. It reflects a lot of care. It might be just a few words, but it's been refined and reviewed by a lot of different people.

And that kind of concision can be challenging, because a lot of tech products are highly technical. Sometimes their underlying dynamics are actually quite confusing and complicated. It's hard to fit it all into a single sentence. Moreover, people don't trust corporate motives. When a company speaks, it generally starts from a low level of credibility. Getting the message through can be difficult.

Part of the reason for that mistrust is that it's rarely in a corporation's interest to be completely honest. In recent years, we've seen a lot of examples of tech companies being less than truthful with the public. Have you ever felt like you needed to tell a story that wasn't completely true?

Well, you always start with the truth. It's the only way. If the truth is that you're launching a new feature to improve advertisers' ability to run ads on your platform, then you start with that. You can't change the purpose of the product, but you can modify where the emphasis is in the explanation.

I never felt pressured to tell a partial truth. But it's not always a question of simple truth or falsity. It's a question of completeness. Every company has a communications component because the message needs to be managed. Why does the message need to be managed? Because if it wasn't, in a company with a hundred thousand employees, you would have a hundred thousand different messages. It's in the interest of the enterprise to have an organized voice.

As for whether that organized voice ever tells an incomplete story—well, that's kind of inherent in the job. As I mentioned earlier, you don't have the airtime to tell a complete story. But I should say, that cuts both ways. Journalists also tell stories about our products, and their stories aren't complete, either. They start with some truths, and inevitably tell their own kind of compelling story.

But isn't there a difference between journalists who may not have all the information but are trying to ascertain the truth as best they can, and companies who are deliberately spinning a story in a particular way?
Look, I would never diminish the value of journalism. Obviously, we need to have journalists out there holding corporations and governments accountable. But every institution has its incentives. And the news media is incentivized for engagement. They need people to click.

One could argue that the tech industry itself is responsible for making the business model of news so focused on engagement. I would say that the dynamic predated the rise of the big platforms, and that the platforms simply accelerated a trend that was already taking place.

Who is Howard Dean? I think about this a lot. Howard Dean is a person who did a lot of stuff. But the only thing that anyone remembers about that guy is that he screamed once. Like, a mic was too loud and it sounded like he was yelling, and his campaign was completely derailed.

Now we live in a media environment where we have a new Dean scream every few minutes. It's an attention economy. The news is designed to attract people's attention and keep it. And what does that well is scandal, controversy, conflict, *House of Cards*–style intrigue. Those are more exciting reads than unadorned facts stitched together to form a much less dramatic reality.

What's the reality?
First off, when things go well, you don't hear about it. When a company launches a feature that's good for users, that nobody finds controversial, it's not covered very widely. That happens all the time.

And when things go wrong, the media narrative doesn't typically capture the complexity of what's happening internally, or the amount of work that's happening behind the scenes. I think journalists sometimes assume that these companies are full of young people who don't understand the seriousness of what they're doing. They're playing Ping-Pong, they're bringing their dogs to work. It's all fun and games.

But in my experience, the challenges that these companies face are not taken lightly at all. The people who work at them, and the executives who run them, are deeply interested in getting it right. The mood is somber, serious.

I'm not sure that the media thinks that the main problem in Silicon Valley is neglect. More often, it seems like the issue is greed—that tech companies are just trying to squeeze out as much profit as they can, no matter what the consequences are.

Perhaps that is how things work at young companies. But at a larger enterprise, nobody wants a short-term gain at the expense of damaging user trust. It's just not worth it.

As humans, we love a good story. And a good story needs heroes and villains. So I understand why the media, and the public more broadly, can be quick to assign malicious motives when a problem arises. But that simply doesn't accord with what I've seen from the inside.

Balancing Acts

You said that the people who work at these companies and the executives who run them understand the seriousness of the issues and what's at stake. Was this

always the case? Or has that understanding emerged more recently, since the various scandals around the 2016 election?

I take umbrage at the idea that Silicon Valley didn't face scrutiny before 2016. When I joined this particular company in 2013, there was already a ton of public attention. And the stakes and the significance of what we were doing were quite clear. That struck me very early on.

To my mind, the techlash has been more a difference of degree than of kind. The scrutiny isn't new. It just became more intense. The stakes became even higher. The year 2016 was clearly an inflection point because tech got bound up with big political issues, with the integrity of a national election, which is a subject that people are very justifiably passionate about.

Let's talk more about that. What's your perspective on the controversies around Russian influence operations during the 2016 election? How do you think the platforms handled it?

People made mistakes. But things that seem obvious now in retrospect just weren't obvious at the time. Or maybe there weren't the right incentives for people to be thinking about the right problems.

Fundamentally, the products were misused. A sovereign nation wanted to interfere with another sovereign nation's elections, and used these platforms to do it. It was cyberwar, basically. These platforms were the weapons, but they were hijacked. Let's say you're an arms manufacturer and your shipment gets hijacked by a hostile country and used to start a war. That's what happened.

But is that really a fair comparison? These platforms make their money from ads, which means they need to maximize engagement. So the business model means they have to prioritize whatever content users find engaging, whether that's Russian disinformation or alt-right propaganda.

With perfect foresight, you could have stopped the Russia stuff from happening—but not without controversy. Those campaigns adopted the idiom of our politically divided country and exaggerated it. So any effort to combat them would have been interpreted as ideological. Let's imagine that the platforms took down a bunch of pro-Trump memes, claiming the Russians put them there. How would Republicans or the Trump campaign have reacted? Critics of misinformation forget that conservatives often accused tech companies of censoring their views before 2016.

It's all about trade-offs. These are the kinds of conversations that happen internally. They're complicated, they take time, they involve a lot of people. There are many considerations: integrity, access to information, community safety, free speech.

Free speech is a big one. The U.S. is where these platforms are based. So they have inherited a lot of norms about free speech and the First Amendment. We pay a price for our love of free speech in the U.S., and that price includes some of the world's most lax defamation laws.

There are plenty of countries where it's a lot easier to sue somebody for defaming you, where satire isn't as well protected, where hate speech laws are stricter—in Europe, for instance, they take a different approach to these questions. But these are American companies, so they tend to take a more maximalist view of free speech. How do you fulfill that expectation at scale while balancing other considerations around safety and accountability?

What if the things that people say cause harm?
Then it has to be dealt with. But what I've seen is that everyone wants it both ways. They want the platforms to be responsible for everything that's said on them, but they also want the platforms to stand down when it's their own speech that might be interfered with. It's just an incredibly challenging thing to get right.

It sounds like you're saying that platforms of a certain scale and significance always face difficult choices that involve trade-offs. But if such trade-offs are inevitable, one could argue that those choices shouldn't be left in the hands of private companies, particularly when the social and political consequences can be so severe. If there are trade-offs that must be made, they should be made through an open, democratic process, using a political forum or a regulatory mechanism of some kind.
If what you're saying is that these kinds of debates should take place in the public arena, then yes, absolutely. There needs to be transparency and accountability. And there's

certainly room for smart regulation by smart governments with the right motives. But personally, based on what I've seen and observed, regulation can be slow-moving. It can be inefficient. It can be counterproductive. And it can cause a whole new set of controversies.

Returning to the Russia question: Fundamentally, the government didn't do its job. Preventing Russian interference in the election should've been the business of the intelligence community from the start. I never personally felt like they were involved. But if they had been, that in itself would have been a different scandal. Imagine people's reaction to finding out the FBI and the CIA or whoever were collaborating closely with the big platforms to combat Russian disinformation. People would freak out about government censorship and surveillance.

Even smart regulation will raise those kinds of concerns. Then, globally, it's a very different picture. Liberals in the U.S. have a tendency to assume that government regulation has our interests at heart. That's not true in many of the more explicitly authoritarian countries where these companies operate.

Another perspective is that, so long as these platforms are private entities trying to maximize profit and shareholder value, they will always be incentivized to put their bottom line over the well-being and interests of their users, and society more broadly.
Well, companies certainly act in their own interests. They have competition. They have to make money to stay in business.

But when I think about how new consumer features come about, it's generally not driven by people thinking about growth or market share in a systematic way. It's certainly not driven by people deliberately thinking about how to take advantage of users. On the contrary: it's usually about people trying to create value for users.

There are different ways to approach that. One is the more extreme, visionary version: You think you know what the world needs. You say, this is how people should interact with each other on the internet, or this is how businesses should do payroll, or whatever.

We might call that the Steve Jobs approach.
Yeah. The other approach is more evidence-driven, which is what I'm more familiar with. It involves gathering data about what people want, what people are frustrated by. At this particular company, it might look like doing research into the pain points of a particular user experience. Then you look for ways to address those concerns.

That incremental development is first and foremost about creating value for users. And sure, if it takes off, business imperatives come into play—how is this going to affect growth, market share, that sort of thing. But that's usually not where it starts. It starts from more of a problem-solving mindset. I would say it's an engineer's approach to the world. It works by identifying friction in existing systems and trying to make them more efficient.

At the end of the day, you need to be building something that people want. You need people to get value from it. Otherwise they won't use it.

That said, with platforms this big, managing that value can get difficult. You have to balance the different considerations we discussed earlier, across many different groups of people at a global scale. You have to find a way to serve one audience while trying not to frustrate or alienate another audience. It's complicated.

Inside Voices

Your job was to tell the public a story about a product. But companies don't just talk to the public—they also talk to themselves. They tell themselves a story about what they're doing, whether in the form of an explicit mission statement or an unofficial mantra. And these internal stories seem especially important in Silicon Valley: don't be evil, move fast and break things, and so on.

Humans need stories. They need to create an accounting for themselves, a sense of how it all fits together. But sometimes people are skeptical about corporate missions or mantras. They think they're too vague or idealistic.

I think of the scene in *Silicon Valley* where all the startup founders are onstage explaining how their complicated technical product is going to "make the world a better place."

Right. The cynical view is that those mantras are a way to get your employees to pretend they're doing something other than building a business. Or, worse, that by permeating the workplace with the language of purpose, you're getting them to be on board with something unpalatable. You can convince them that whatever bad thing they're doing is for a cause. At the end of the day, very few people in their self-accounting are comfortable with thinking of themselves as deliberately inflicting harm. So those missions might be seen as a form of rationalization, as a way for the company to engage in "cause washing."

The more charitable view is that those phrases can actually help lead to the right outcomes. I've seen a lot of situations where the mission has been invoked at a critical juncture and it's helped refocus things in the right direction.

What's an example?
Within a company, people are incentivized for their own success. They have to perform, they have goals. It's natural. But that can mean that in a group setting, they will argue for the things that will eventually make them look good. They will focus on their own self-interest, their own targets, and their own achievements.

I've seen the mission work in a way that counters those dynamics. It helps reground the conversation. It helps people pull back from the individual incentives and ask, "What are we doing here?"

The whole change-the-world mentality that these mantras embody can certainly feel impractical or utopian—and we're in an era now where we're second-guessing it—but as a working model I've definitely seen it improve outcomes rather than degrade them.

So missions or mantras can be useful for reorienting away from the individual to the collective—away from an employee who's trying to maximize their opportunity to thinking at the level of the team or the firm as a whole.

Yeah. And that's why they *have* to be lofty. Creating a sense of shared purpose is the whole point of these things.

You can have either a cynical or a charitable interpretation of their existence. You could ask what would be different about these companies if you subtracted their missions or mantras. And in my view, the difference is there'd be a little less sense of purpose, and without a sense of purpose, things would be harder. You've gotta have everybody rowing in the same direction.

We've talked about the story the company tells about a product, and the story the company tells itself about what it's doing. But what about the story that you personally tell about your own work, to friends, family, or others? Has telling that story become harder in recent years, as the scrutiny of these companies has grown more intense?

I'm not interested in being an apologist for corporate or industry interests. So the conversation I would have with friends or family, or even a stranger in a bar, is not too different from what we've talked about here.

Basically, I think the truth is important. The public conversation about tech can sometimes fall into a simplistic framework: the industry increasingly feels like it's being put in the same category as Big Oil or Big Tobacco. And I think the industry has had a lot of growing up to do, but it doesn't strike me as that simple. These products can be misused, but they aren't carcinogens.

So in those conversations, I try to go beyond the hype and talk specifics. What is the specific situation and what are the specific challenges? If people are upset about Russia, or the mismanagement of user expectations with a new product launch, well, that's a real concern. That's something they should be upset about, and the company should respond to it. They're entitled to not like a feature or a product, they're entitled not to use it.

Probably the most frequent thing you hear when you say you work at one of these tech companies is people telling you, somewhat contemptuously and smugly, that they don't use the product. "Oh, I don't have that anymore." "I don't like that." It's almost like they're trying to goad you into selling them on why they should use it. And I always find it a bit strange, because I really don't care. I totally understand. If someone doesn't want to use something, they don't have to. That doesn't bother me at all.

Why did you stop doing this job? What prompted that decision?
I kind of burned out. Not necessarily with the company or the industry, but with my role. Burnout is a big thing in

the industry. It's a burnout culture. The companies have gotten a bit better in trying to help people balance things better, but still, the work takes a toll.

For me personally, I think I lost faith in words. I felt fed up with the mandate of merely talking, because in my heart I don't think that the words about things matter as much as the things themselves.

Why not?
Because the words don't feel so effective. It's been a tough few years. With the challenges we've been discussing, it can feel frustrating if all you're doing is talking. There are communicators and there are builders. I'd like to spend my time building products rather than telling stories about them. There is no shortage of problems, and I'd like to help solve them. There are limits to talking.

Acknowledgments

This book would not have been possible without the people whose voices fill its pages. We're grateful to them for speaking with us and letting us share their stories.

We're also indebted to Chris Parris-Lamb for providing crucial encouragement early on, and to Emily Bell, Jackson Howard, and everyone at FSG Originals for taking a chance on this collaboration. To Zoe Tarnoff, for slowing us down. And, above all, to the other members of our *Logic* family: Jim Fingal, Christa Hartsock, Xiaowei Wang, Celine Nguyen, Jen Kagan, and Alex Blasdel. Without their wisdom and kindness, this book—and much more—would not exist.